Introducing GitHub
A Non-Technical Guide

Peter Bell and Brent Beer

Beijing · Cambridge · Farnham · Köln · Sebastopol · Tokyo

Introducing GitHub

by Peter Bell and Brent Beer

Copyright © 2015 Pragmatic Learning, Inc. All rights reserved.

Printed in the United States of America.

Published by O'Reilly Media, Inc., 1005 Gravenstein Highway North, Sebastopol, CA 95472.

O'Reilly books may be purchased for educational, business, or sales promotional use. Online editions are also available for most titles (*http://safaribooksonline.com*). For more information, contact our corporate/institutional sales department: 800-998-9938 or *corporate@oreilly.com*.

Editor: Meghan Blanchette	**Indexer:** Judy McConville
Production Editor: Melanie Yarbrough	**Interior Designer:** David Futato
Copyeditor: Sonia Saruba	**Cover Designer:** Karen Montgomery
Proofreader: Sharon Wilkey	**Illustrator:** Rebecca Demarest

November 2014:   First Edition

Revision History for the First Edition

2014-11-07:   First Release

See *http://oreilly.com/catalog/errata.csp?isbn=9781491949740* for release details.

The O'Reilly logo is a registered trademark of O'Reilly Media, Inc. *Introducing GitHub*, the cover image, and related trade dress are trademarks of O'Reilly Media, Inc.

While the publisher and the authors have used good faith efforts to ensure that the information and instructions contained in this work are accurate, the publisher and the authors disclaim all responsibility for errors or omissions, including without limitation responsibility for damages resulting from the use of or reliance on this work. Use of the information and instructions contained in this work is at your own risk. If any code samples or other technology this work contains or describes is subject to open source licenses or the intellectual property rights of others, it is your responsibility to ensure that your use thereof complies with such licenses and/or rights.

978-1-491-94974-0

[LSI]

Table of Contents

Preface

GitHub is changing the way that software gets built. Conceived originally as a way to make it easier for developers to contribute to open source projects, GitHub is rapidly becoming the default platform for software development. More than just a tool for storing source code, GitHub provides a range of powerful tools for specifying, discussing, and reviewing software.

Who This Book Is For

If you are working with developers on a software project, this book is for you, whether you are a:

- *Business stakeholder* who wants to have a sense of how your project is going
- *Product or project manager* who needs to ensure that software is delivered on time and within budget
- *Designer* who needs to deliver anything from mockups to HTML/CSS for a project
- *Copywriter* who's adding marketing copy or other content to a site or an app
- *Lawyer* who's reviewing the legal implications of a project or writing the terms and conditions or privacy policy
- *Team member* who needs to review, comment on, and/or contribute to the project
- *Developer* who is new to using GitHub and wants to learn how to collaborate using GitHub in a team

If you need to view the progress of a piece of software while it's being developed, if you would like to be able to comment on the progress, and if you'd like to have the option of contributing changes to the project, this book will show you how to effectively collaborate with a software development team by using GitHub.

Beyond Software

While GitHub is still primarily used to collaborate on the development of software, it's also a great way for a team to collaborate on a wide range of projects. From the authoring of books (like this one) and the distribution of models for 3D printing to the crafting of legislation, whenever you have a team of people collaborating on a collection of documents, you should consider using GitHub to manage the process. Our examples will assume that you're working on software because that is currently the most common use case, but this book is the perfect guide to collaborating via GitHub —whatever kind of project you're working on.

Who This Book Is Not For

This book is designed to teach the core skills required to collaborate effectively using GitHub. If you are already familiar with forking, cloning, and using feature branches and pull requests for collaboration, you probably won't learn that much.

Equally, if you are looking for an in-depth introduction to the Git version control system, this is not the book that you are looking for. This book covers just enough Git to do the job of introducing GitHub, but it's not a comprehensive introduction to Git. For that you should read the excellent *Version Control with Git* by Jon Loeliger and Matthew McCullough (O'Reilly, 2012).

How to Use This Book

We've deliberately made this book as concise as possible. You should be able to read it pretty quickly. If you want to gain the confidence that comes from really understanding what GitHub is about and how to use it, try to read the book from start to finish.

However, we know that you're busy. If you're in a rush, start by skimming the first chapter. Chapter 1 gives you a brief introduction to Git, GitHub, and some key terms that you'll need to understand to make sense of the rest of the book. Then feel free to just jump into whatever chapters you need. We've tried to write the book so that each chapter runs you through specific workflows, so you should be able to read just the chapter you need to complete a particular task.

Conventions Used in This Book

The following typographical conventions are used in this book:

Italic
> Indicates new terms, URLs, email addresses, filenames, and file extensions.

Constant width

Used for program listings, as well as within paragraphs to refer to program elements such as variable or function names, databases, data types, environment variables, statements, and keywords.

Constant width bold

Shows commands or other text that should be typed literally by the user.

Constant width italic

Shows text that should be replaced with user-supplied values or by values determined by context.

 This element signifies a tip or suggestion.

 This element signifies a general note.

 This element indicates a warning or caution.

Safari® Books Online

 *Safari Books Online* is an on-demand digital library that delivers expert content in both book and video form from the world's leading authors in technology and business.

Technology professionals, software developers, web designers, and business and creative professionals use Safari Books Online as their primary resource for research, problem solving, learning, and certification training.

Safari Books Online offers a range of plans and pricing for enterprise, government, education, and individuals.

Members have access to thousands of books, training videos, and prepublication manuscripts in one fully searchable database from publishers like O'Reilly Media, Prentice Hall Professional, Addison-Wesley Professional, Microsoft Press, Sams, Que, Peachpit Press, Focal Press, Cisco Press, John Wiley & Sons, Syngress, Morgan Kaufmann, IBM Redbooks, Packt, Adobe Press, FT Press, Apress, Manning, New Riders, McGraw-Hill, Jones & Bartlett, Course Technology, and hundreds more. For more information about Safari Books Online, please visit us online.

How to Contact Us

Please address comments and questions concerning this book to the publisher:

O'Reilly Media, Inc.
1005 Gravenstein Highway North
Sebastopol, CA 95472
800-998-9938 (in the United States or Canada)
707-829-0515 (international or local)
707-829-0104 (fax)

We have a web page for this book, where we list errata, examples, and any additional information. You can access this page at *http://bit.ly/intro-github*.

To comment or ask technical questions about this book, send email to *bookquestions@oreilly.com*.

For more information about our books, courses, conferences, and news, see our website at *http://www.oreilly.com*.

Find us on Facebook: *http://facebook.com/oreilly*

Follow us on Twitter: *http://twitter.com/oreillymedia*

Watch us on YouTube: *http://www.youtube.com/oreillymedia*

Acknowledgments

Peter: I would like to thank my wife for her tireless support of the time and effort required to write this book—and the many other projects that keep me away from her more than I'd like that don't have acknowledgments sections! I would also like to thank my Mum for always going above and beyond to give me the support I needed to always follow my dreams—even under often difficult circumstances.

Brent: I'd like to thank my Mom for her constant encouragement for reading, without which I may never have found a love for it. And also my Dad. Without him letting me watch him work on our computer, entertaining me with the Oscar the Grouch trash can utility on our Macintosh, and encouraging me to learn how to program, I would not be in the field I am today.

We would both like to thank the inspiring Matthew and Jordan McCullough and the rest of the GitHub team for their feedback on this book and their ideas and support over the years. Much of the best content here came from them. We'd also like to thank the amazing Meg Blanchette at O'Reilly, without whom this book would never have been conceived, written, or delivered—thanks so much, Meg!

CHAPTER 1

Introduction

In this chapter we'll start by introducing Git and GitHub. What are they, what is the difference between them, and why would you want to use them? We'll then introduce some other common terms that you'll often hear mentioned when people are discussing GitHub. That way you'll be able to understand and participate in discussions about your projects more easily.

What Is Git?

Git is a version control system. A *version control system* is a piece of software designed to keep track of the changes made to files over time. More specifically, Git is a *distributed* version control system, which means that everyone working with a project in Git has a copy of the full history of the project, not just the current state of the files.

What Is GitHub?

GitHub is a website where you can upload a copy of your Git repository. It allows you to collaborate much more easily with other people on a project. It does that by providing a centralized location to share the repository, a web-based interface to view it, and features like *forking*, *pull requests*, *issues*, and *wikis*, which allow you to specify, discuss, and review changes with your team more effectively.

Why Use Git?

Even if you're working on your own, if you are editing text files, there are a number of benefits to using Git. Those benefits include the following:

The ability to undo changes
> If you make a mistake, you can go back to a previous point in time to recover an earlier version of your work.

A complete history of all the changes
> If you ever want to see what your project looked like a day, week, month, or year ago, you can *check out* a previous version of the project to see exactly what the state of the files was back then.

Documentation of why changes were made
> Often it's hard to remember *why* a change was made. With *commit messages* in Git, it's easy to document for future reference why you're making a change.

The confidence to change anything
> Because it's easy to recover a previous version of your project, you can have the confidence to make any changes you want. If they don't work out, you can always get back to an earlier version of your work.

Multiple streams of history
> You can create different *branches* of history to experiment with different changes to your content or to build out different features independently. You can then *merge* those back into the main project history (the *master branch*) once they're done, or delete them if they end up not working out.

Working on a team, you get an even wider range of benefits when using Git to keep track of your changes. Some of the key benefits of Git when working with a team are:

The ability to resolve conflicts
> With Git, multiple people can work on the same file at the same time. Usually Git will be able to merge the changes automatically. If it can't, it'll show you what the conflicts are and will make it easy for you to resolve them.

Independent streams of history
> Different people on the project can work on different *branches*, allowing you to work on separate features independently and then merge the features when they're done.

Why Use GitHub?

GitHub is much more than just a place to store your Git repositories. It provides a number of additional benefits, including the ability to do the following:

Document requirements
> Using *Issues*, you can either document bugs or specify new features that you'd like to have your team develop.

Collaborate on independent streams of history
> Using branches and *pull requests*, you can collaborate on different branches or features.

Review work in progress

By looking at a list of pull requests, you can see all of the different features that are currently being worked on, and by clicking any given pull request, you can see the latest changes as well as all of the discussions about the changes.

See team progress

Skimming the *pulse* or looking through the *commit history* allows you to see what the team has been working on.

Key Concepts

There are a number of key concepts that you'll need to understand to work effectively with Git and GitHub. Here is a list of some of the most common terms with a short description of each and an example of how they might be used in conversation:

Commit

Whenever you save your changes to one or more files to history in Git, you create a new commit. *Example usage: "Let's commit these changes and push them up to GitHub."*

Commit message

Every time you make a commit, you need to supply a message that describes *why* the change was made. That commit message is invaluable when trying to understand later why a certain change was implemented. *Example usage: "Make sure to include Susan's comment about the new SEC guidelines in the commit message."*

Branch

An independent series of commits off to one side that you can use to try out an experiment or create a new feature. *Example usage: "Let's create a branch to implement the new search functionality."*

Master branch (master)

Whenever you create a new Git project, there is a default branch created that is called *master*. This is the branch that your work should end up on eventually once it's ready to push to production. *Example usage: "Remember never to commit directly to master."*

Feature (or topic) branch

Whenever you're building a new piece of functionality, you'll create a branch to work on it. That's called a *feature branch. Example usage: "We've got way too many feature branches. Let's focus on getting one or two of these finished and into production."*

Release branch

If you have a manual QA process or have to support old versions of your software for your customers, you might need a release branch as a place to make any necessary fixes or updates. There is no technical difference between a feature or release branch, but the distinction is useful when talking about a project with your team. *Example usage: "We've got to fix the security bug on all of our supported release branches."*

Merge

This is a way to take completed work from one branch and incorporate it into another branch. Most commonly you'll merge a feature branch into the master branch. *Example usage: "Great job on the 'my account' feature. Could you merge it into master so we can push it to production?"*

Tag

A reference to a specific historic commit. Most often used to document production releases so you know exactly which versions of the code went into production and when. *Example usage: "Let's tag this release and push it to production."*

Check out

To go to a different version of the project's history to see the files as of that point in time. Most commonly you'll check out a branch to see all of the work that has been done on it, but any commit can be checked out. *Example usage: "Could you check out the last release tag? There's a bug in production that I need you to replicate and fix."*

Pull request

Originally, a pull request was used to request that someone else review the work you completed on a branch and then merge it into master. Now, pull requests are often used earlier in the process to start a discussion about a possible feature. *Example usage: "Go create a pull request for the new voting feature so we can see what the rest of the team thinks about it."*

Issue

GitHub has a feature called Issues that can be used to discuss features, track bugs, or both. *Example usage: "You're right, the login doesn't work on an iPhone. Could you create an issue on GitHub documenting the steps to replicate the bug?"*

Wiki

Originally developed by Ward Cunningham, wikis are a lightweight way of creating web pages with simple links between them. GitHub projects often use wikis for documentation. *Example usage: "Could you add a page to the wiki to explain how to configure the project to run on multiple servers?"*

Clone

Often you'll want to download a copy of a project from GitHub so you can work on it locally. The process of copying the repository to your computer is called *cloning*. *Example usage: "Could you clone the repo, fix the bug, and then push the fix back up to GitHub later tonight?"*

Fork

Sometimes you don't have the necessary permission to make changes directly to a project. Perhaps it's an open source project written by people you don't know or it's a project written by another group at your company that you don't work with much. If you want to submit changes to such a project, first you need to make a copy of the project under *your* user account on GitHub. That process is called *forking* the repository. You can then clone it, make changes, and submit them back to the original project using a pull request. *Example usage: "I'd love to see how you'd rewrite the home page marketing copy. Fork the repo and submit a pull request with your proposed changes."*

Don't worry if all the terminology seems overwhelming at first. Once you start working with some real projects, it'll all make a lot more sense! In the next chapter we'll look at the various elements of a GitHub project and how you can use them to get a sense of progress on a project.

CHAPTER 2

Viewing

In this chapter we'll look at how you can view the state of a project to see what's going on. We'll use the popular Bootstrap open source project as an example (*http://getboot strap.com/*).

Introducing the Project Page

Bootstrap is a project that allows developers to quickly develop attractive web applications. Go to the project page on GitHub (*https://github.com/twbs/bootstrap*). There is a lot of information on the home page. Let's start by reviewing some of the most important elements on the page (see Figure 2-1).

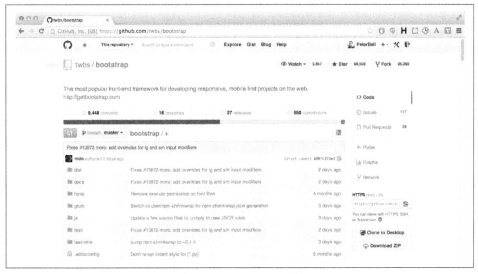

Figure 2-1. The Bootstrap project home page on GitHub

One of the first things you see looking at the top left of the page is that the project name is "bootstrap" and that it's owned by a user (or in this case an organization) called "twbs." If you were to go to *https://github.com/twbs*, you'd see a list of all of the projects hosted by that organization at GitHub. To the left of the organization name you'll also see an icon that makes it clear that this is a public repository that anyone can see. A lot of the projects you work on will have a closed lock icon instead, signifying that they are private and can be viewed only by people who have been explicitly added as collaborators.

To the right of the project name, you can see in Figure 2-1 that at the time the screenshot was taken, 3,857 people were *watching* the repository to get notified every time new changes were made to it, 68,928 people had *starred* it to mark it as one of their favorite projects, and 25,292 people had *forked* the repository, making their own copy on GitHub where they could upload changes to the project and share them with others.

Further down the page, you can see a short description of the project, and below that you'll see that there have been a total of 9,448 changes to the project (commits), 16 different streams of history are currently being developed (branches), 27 versions of the software have been recommended over time for people to use (releases), and 550 people wrote some part of the code (contributors).

You can also see that we're currently viewing the master branch, that we're in the root *bootstrap* folder, that the latest commit on master was "Fixes #13872 more: add overrides for lg and sm input modifiers" (whatever that means), and that the commit was made by GitHub user "mdo." (*https://github.com/mdo*) As you look further down the figure, you can see the folders (sometimes called *directories*) and files that are in the root (top-level) folder in the project.

Viewing the README.md File

If there is a file in the root of a project named *README.md*, the contents of that file will be displayed just below the list of folders and files on the project home page. This file provides an introduction to the project and additional information that would be useful to collaborators, such as how to install the software, how to run any automated tests, how to use the code, and how to make contributions to the project.

These days, README files will often also include badges—images used to show the current state of things, like the automated test suite to let you know the current state of the project. In Figure 2-2, the Bootstrap project is showing the version of two other projects that Bootstrap depends on. It's also showing that the automated tests are passing, that the dependencies are up-to-date, and the versions of browsers and operating systems that Bootstrap should work for.

Figure 2-2. The contents of the Bootstrap project's README.md file

Viewing the Commit History

The commit history is a great way to get a sense of the most recent small units of work that have been completed on any given branch. Go to the Bootstrap page on GitHub (*https://github.com/twbs/bootstrap*) and click the "9,448 commits" link (the number of commits will have changed by the time you do this). You'll see a list of commits—most recent first (see Figure 2-3).

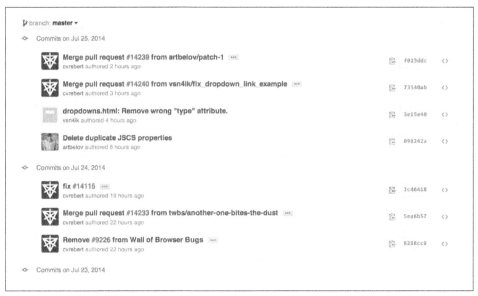

Figure 2-3. A list of the recent commits on the project

Clicking any of the commits will show you the commit message that should explain *why* the changes were made. Below that you will see each file that was added, removed, or modified as part of the commit, with content that was removed displaying in red and content that was added displaying in green (see Figure 2-4).

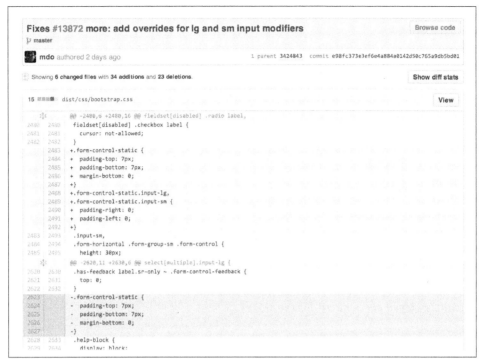

Figure 2-4. A recent commit on the project

Viewing Pull Requests

Pull requests give you a sense of the current work in progress. Go back to the home page and click the "Pull requests" link in the top-right and you'll see a list of open pull requests. These are the outstanding features or fixes that people are currently working on (see Figure 2-5).

Figure 2-5. Open pull requests for the project

Click one of the pull requests and you'll see a short title describing the pull request. There are one or more commits with the proposed changes, and there may be a number of comments from people discussing the proposed changes (see Figure 2-6).

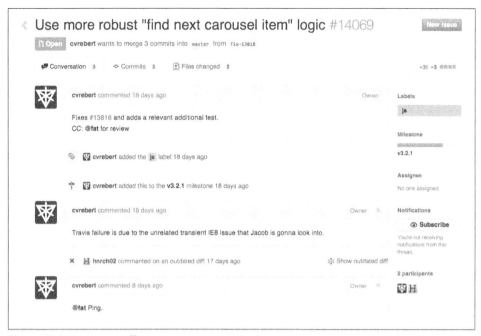

Figure 2-6. A recent pull request

Looking at the pull requests is a great way to get a sense of what people are working on now and the current state of play of each of those changes—whether bug fixes or proposed features.

Viewing Issues

While pull requests give you a sense of the current bug fixes and features being worked on, issues can give you a wider sense of the outstanding work that still needs to be done on a project. Pull requests are often linked to an issue, but there will usually also be issues that nobody has started working on yet, so they don't yet have a pull request.

If you click the link to view the list of issues, by default you'll see a list of all of the open issues (see Figure 2-7).

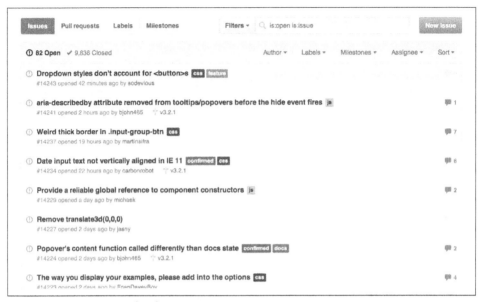

Figure 2-7. Open issues for the project

Click an issue and you'll see the title and any comments related to the issue. If any work has been done and pushed to GitHub, and if the commit message references an issue, it'll show up on the Issue page so you can see what's being done. In Figure 2-8 someone appears to be having a problem with one of the Bootstrap features.

Figure 2-8. A recent issue

Viewing the Pulse

The *pulse* is a great way to get a sense for the recent activity on a project. Notice in the top right of Figure 2-9 that you can customize the pulse to be for the last day, three days, week, or month.

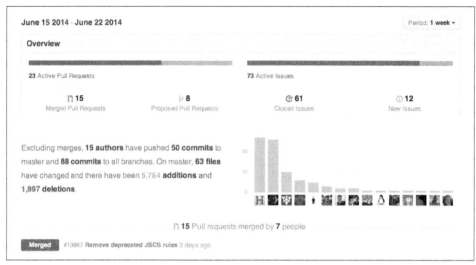

Figure 2-9. The pulse for Bootstrap

The pulse starts with an overview of the number of pull requests that have been merged (completed) and proposed (added). It also shows how many issues were closed or opened. It's important to understand that when the pulse refers to the number of active pull requests and issues, this is not the outstanding number of each but rather the number of requests and issues that have been started and finished in the time period you selected. For example, at the time of writing, Bootstrap had 15 merged and 8 proposed pull requests for a total of 23 "active" pull requests in the last week, but it had a total of 28 open pull requests.

The next paragraph on the screen is a concise summary of recent changes, listing the number of authors, commits on master, total commits on all branches, and the number of files added, removed, or modified on the master branch. It then gives you the number of lines of content that have been added or removed, although it's important to realize that if a line of text in a file is modified, Git will treat it as if one line was removed and another different line was added in its place.

To the right is a bar chart showing the contributors who have made the most commits during the period. Below that is a list of the titles of the merged and proposed pull requests, followed by the closed and then opened issues. The pulse view ends with a list of "unresolved conversations," which is a list of all of the issues and pull requests that have received additional comments but have not yet been closed.

Viewing GitHub Graphs

While the pulse gives you a summary of recent activity, the graph pages allow you to get a sense of the work that has been done on a project over a longer period of time.

The Contributors Graph

The contributors graph in Figure 2-10 shows you the number of contributions over time based on the number of commits, additions, or deletions. It shows a graph for all of the contributions, followed by smaller graphs showing the contributions by the individual developers—from the most to the least prolific.

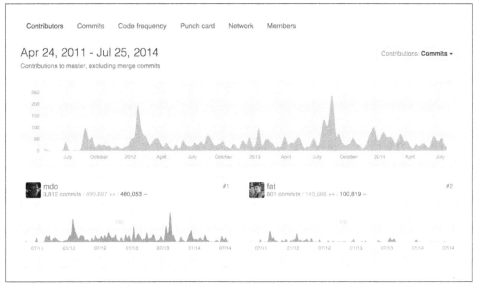

Figure 2-10. The contributors graph for Bootstrap

The default commits graph shows the number of commits that have been made over time to the master branch. It's important to realize that it shows only the commits that have been merged into the master branch. If you have someone on your team who has been working on a feature branch all week and whose work has not yet been merged in, none of those contributions will show up until they are ready for release and have been merged into the master branch.

By default, the time period for the graph is the entire lifetime of the project. If you'd like to pick a shorter time, just click the starting point you'd like on the main graph and then drag and release on the time you'd like the new graph to end. Figure 2-11 shows the results of doing this to focus on the commits over the summer of 2013. You can see that the main graph at the top of the page stays the same, but at the top-left it shows the time period we're focused on (June 30 through September 2). The commit graphs of the individual contributors shows the number of commits and how they were spread out over that time period.

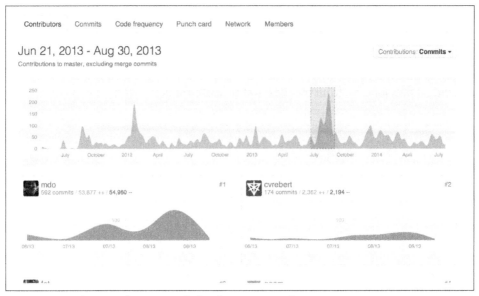

Figure 2-11. The contributors graph for the summer of 2013

There is no standard size for a commit. A good rule of thumb is that if developers are writing code as opposed to researching a problem or testing something, they should probably be committing every 5 to 10 minutes. However, depending on the team you're working with, you might find that some developers create many fewer commits than others, even if they're doing a similar amount of work. If that is the case, you might want to change the "contribution type" for your contributor graphs to additions or deletions. In that way, you'll get a sense of the number of lines of code that the developers have added or removed from the project. If they modify a line, it will show up as a deletion of the old line and an addition of the new one.

The Commits Graph

The commits graph in Figure 2-12 shows the number of commits per week over the life of the project, giving a very rough proxy for activity and how it has varied over time.

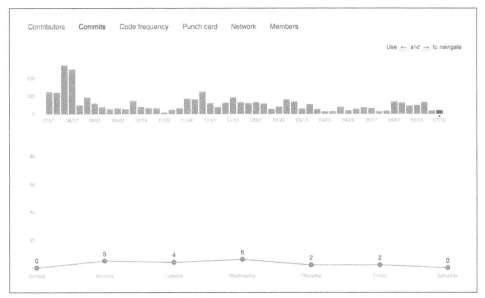

Figure 2-12. The commits graph for Bootstrap

The first reason to look at the commits graph is to get a sense of how many commits per week there have been over the lifetime of the project. It starts with a bar graph showing one bar per week and is a great way to see cyclical or long-term trends. Is the number of commits in your project slowly decreasing? If you have more developers, is the number of commits consistently increasing? Are most of your commits in the last week of every month, or are there seasonal trends? This graph can give you good insight into how the number of commits—which is a very rough proxy for productivity—are varying over time.

Below the bar graph is a line graph showing the average number of commits on each day of the week over the lifetime of the project. This graph can be useful for getting a sense of the cadence over the course of an average week. Are people not committing on Mondays because of too many meetings? Are they making most of their commits on a Thursday ahead of your Friday "demo days," or are they working too much on the weekend, which isn't good for long-term sustainability?

The Code Frequency Graph

The code frequency graph in Figure 2-13 shows you the number of lines added to and removed from your project over time and is particularly helpful for identifying large changes to your code base.

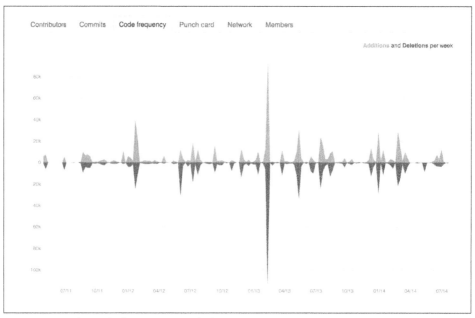

Figure 2-13. The code frequency graph for Bootstrap

The code frequency graph is a great way to see when there have been big changes on your project. Often when developers are doing a big refactoring, they'll add and delete hundreds or even thousands of lines of code per commit, whereas in the usual course of business, a commit will probably contain only a few lines of added, modified, or deleted code. When such a refactoring is going on, the number of commits might not change much, but the number of lines added and deleted will spike, so if you want to get a sense of when the biggest changes happened to your code base, you should start by having a look at the code frequency graph. For example, you can see in Figure 2-13 that a big refactoring was done in February and March of 2013.

The Punch Card Graph

The punch card graph in Figure 2-14 shows what time of day and which day most commits get done.

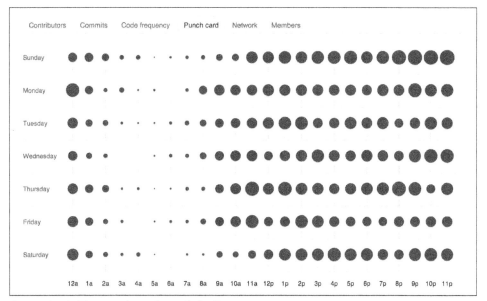

Figure 2-14. The punch card graph for Bootstrap

The punch card graph displays a circle for every hour of every day in the week. The diameters of the circles are a function of the percentage of the commits for the project made during that hour on that day. The bigger the circle, the more of your project commits have been made at that time. Again, this a great way to get insight into the times when your team is most productive.

The Network Graph

The network graph in Figure 2-15 shows the number of branches and commits on those branches throughout a project's history. It also shows any forks that contributors have created.

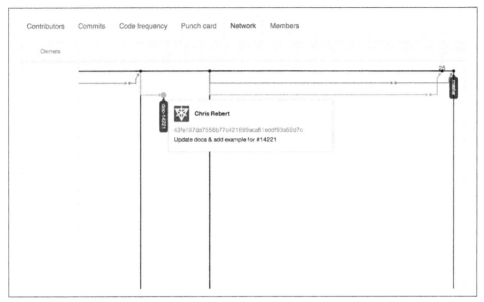

Figure 2-15. The network graph

The network graph is useful for seeing how far ahead one branch may be, or what kind of work someone may be working on in their own fork. When these commits make their way back into the original repository's master, we'll see this come in with an arrow and a merge commit if it was done via a pull request. We can also mouse over these commits to see who wrote them and what the commit message was.

The Members List

The last graph that everyone can see regardless of permissions is the members list. If there is an unusual number of forks, we'll see a message like the one in Figure 2-16, displaying only a partial list of members.

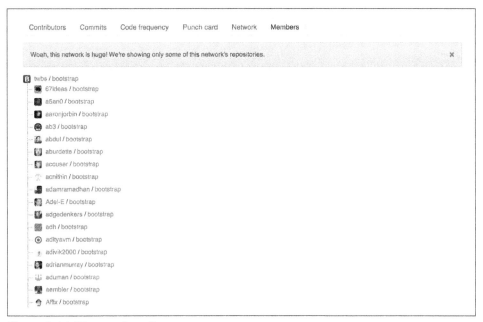

Figure 2-16. The members list

The members list shows just the people who have forked the repository or forks of forks. These people aren't collaborators on the original parent repository and therefore needed their own copy of the repository in order to contribute to it through a pull request.

The Traffic Graph

One additional graph, which is available only to owners and collaborators on a project, is the traffic graph shown in Figure 2-17.

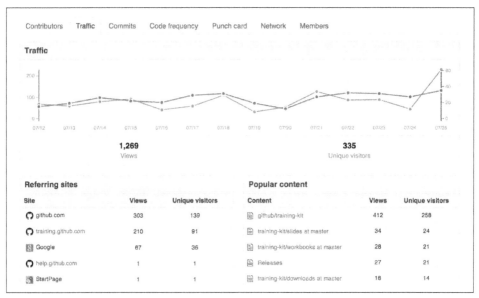

Figure 2-17. The traffic graph

The traffic graph shows you the number of views and unique visitors over time, lists the sites that people are linking from, and highlights the most popular content on your GitHub project site. It can be a great way to get a sense of the popularity for open source projects.

By now you should have a good sense of how to get up to speed with a project by looking at the README file, commits, pull requests, issues, the pulse, and the Git-Hub graphs. In the next chapter we'll look at how you can start to contribute to a project.

CHAPTER 3

Editing

In this chapter we'll look at how you can contribute to a project. We'll start by looking at how to contribute to a project that you don't have permission to push to by creating a fork and a pull request. We'll then look at how you can add, edit, rename, or delete a file directly on GitHub. We'll also look at how to work with directories on GitHub, and finally we'll discuss what to do when you want to make multiple changes as part of a single commit.

Contributing via a Fork

If you want to contribute directly to a project, you either need to own it or have been added to it as a collaborator. If you want to contribute to a project that you don't own and are not a collaborator on, you'll need to make a copy of it on GitHub under your user account. That process is called *forking*. Once you've forked a project, you'll be able to make any changes you want to your fork (copy) and you'll be able to request that your changes get incorporated into the original project by using a pull request. Let's go through that process now.

Go to *https://github.com/pragmaticlearning/github-example*. Click the Fork button in the top right corner of the page, as shown in Figure 3-1.

Figure 3-1. The Fork button

When you click the Fork button, if you are a member of any organizations, you'll see a list of all of the organizations you're involved with as well as your username. You'll be asked where you want to fork the repository. Figure 3-2 shows what that dialog looks like.

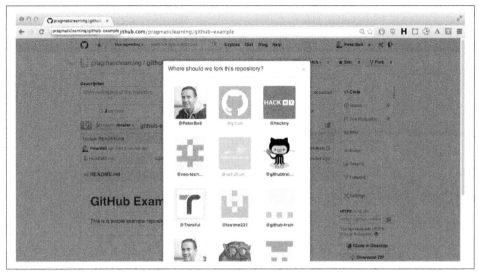

Figure 3-2. Selecting where to fork a repo

After you select where you want to fork the repository (repo), or if you are not a member of any organizations, you'll be taken to your new project page. Once you've forked the repo, you can make any changes you want to your fork (copy). In the next section we'll look at how you can add a new file, and then how to create a pull request to try to get your change incorporated into the original project.

Adding a File

In this section we'll look at how to add a new file to a project. As you can see in Figure 3-3, there is a small plus sign (+) to the right of the project name.

Figure 3-3. The "add new file" link

Click the plus sign and you'll be taken to a screen in Figure 3-4.

Figure 3-4. The "add new file" screen

Toward the top of the page is a text box just to the right of the project name, where you can enter the name of the file you want to add to the project. Below that is a text area where you can enter the content you'd like to put in the file. Scroll down the page when you're done naming the file and entering the content, and as shown in Figure 3-5, you'll see a couple of text boxes where you can create a (required) short description and an optional extended description of the change that you're making.

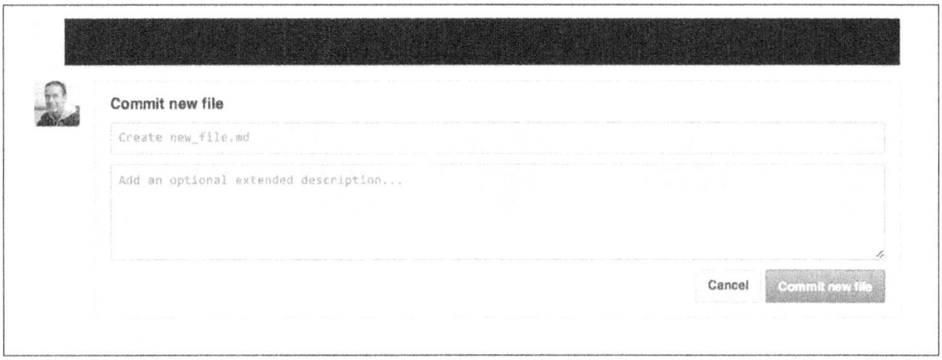

Commit new file

Create new_file.md

Add an optional extended description...

Cancel   Commit new file

Figure 3-5. The bottom of the "add new file" screen

These descriptions will be saved as the commit message for your commit. If you don't enter anything, the default commit message will be "Create (*filename*)." Generally, you'll want to enter a meaningful commit message so other people viewing the project will understand what you did and why you did it. Click the green "Commit new file" button, and your new file will be added to the project and your commit will be added to the commit history. You can see in Figure 3-6 that *new_file.md* has been added to the list of files and that, in my case, there are now three commits—the latest of which is the commit I just made by adding this file.

Figure 3-6. The project home page after adding the new file

Creating a Pull Request

We've made a change to our fork of the project, but the change hasn't propagated back to the original project. That makes sense. Anyone can fork any public project, and the project owner wouldn't want just anyone editing all of their files. However, sometimes it's great to allow other people to *propose* changes to a project. This allows a large number of people to easily contribute to an open source project or a smaller team to work together on an internal project. That is what pull requests are for.

With a pull request, you can request that changes you've made on a fork be incorporated into the original project. Let's go through the process now. As you can see in Figure 3-7, on the right side of the page there is a Pull Requests tab.

Figure 3-7. The Pull Requests tab on the project home page

Click the Pull Requests tab, and you'll see a screen similar to Figure 3-8 showing that currently you don't have any outstanding pull requests. Click the green "New pull request" button at the top right of the screen.

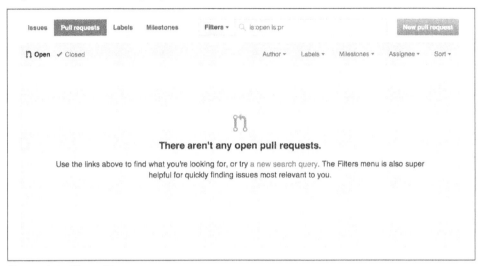

Figure 3-8. *The pull requests screen*

When you click the button, you'll see a screen similar to Figure 3-9.

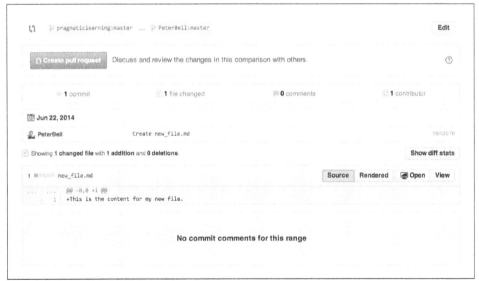

Figure 3-9. *The "preview pull request" screen*

One of the first things you see in Figure 3-9 is that it is proposing a pull request between pragmaticlearning:master and PeterBell:master. Pull requests are requests to incorporate the changes from one branch (stream of history) into another. In this case, GitHub has correctly guessed that I want to take the change that I made on the master branch on my fork (the new file I added) and have that merged back into the master branch on the original project that I forked from. Note that the branch with the changes that you want merged in is on the right, and the target branch you'd like it to be merged into is on the left.

As you look lower down on Figure 3-9, you'll also see that it provides a summary of the changes that would occur if that pull request was merged—I did indeed make one commit that changed a single file. It even shows in green the new content that would be added to *new_file.md*. If I click the "Show diff stats" button, it would even show numerically that one line of content was being added and no lines of content were being removed.

Once we've confirmed that the proposed pull request is the one we want to create, the next step is to click the large green "Create pull request" button. Doing so will take you to a page similar to Figure 3-10.

Figure 3-10. The "create pull request" screen

This screen is your chance to tell the story about why your changes should be incorporated in the other project, so take the time to create a meaningful title and description of the changes you've made. By default the title will be the first line of your commit message for your most recent commit, and if you've made more than one commit on the branch you're trying to have merged, the description will have a bulleted list of the first line of all of the commit messages that are part of the pull request. That's a fine starting point, but you're going to want to take a little bit of time to describe not only what changes you've made, but why you made them and why they'd be a good addition to the project.

Once you've finished describing your pull request, click the "Create pull request" button and you'll see a page that looks like Figure 3-11.

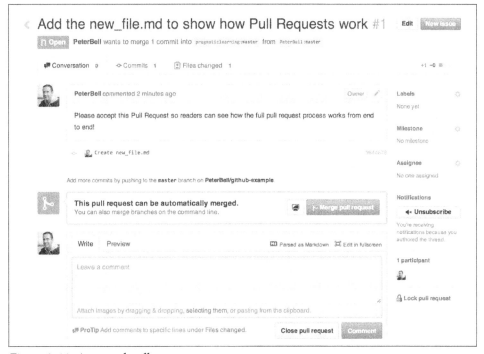

Figure 3-11. A created pull request

There are a couple of things that you should notice in Figure 3-11. First, notice that we're now in the original project—under pragmaticlearning. This makes sense. We wanted to create a request to pull our work into that project, so the pull request is part of that project—not our fork. You can see that "PeterBell wants to merge 1 commit into pragmaticlearning:master from PeterBell:master," and it shows you the pull request (title and description) followed by the commit that was made. Clicking that commit displays the details of the commit, as you can see in Figure 3-12.

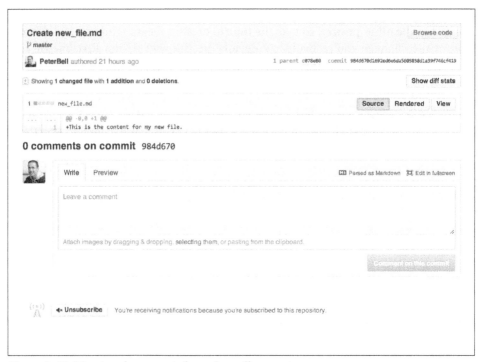

Figure 3-12. Viewing the commit from the pull request

Notice that the commit link has taken us back to the PeterBell version of the repo because that is where the commit was made. It shows you the commit message, who made the change, and the changes that were introduced in that commit.

Going back to the pull request in Figure 3-11, you'll see that there is an option to merge the pull request. That option is visible only to the owner of the project or to anyone the owner has added as collaborators. If someone without those permissions was looking at the page, he would not be able to merge the pull request. For example, in Figure 3-13 I've logged in as another user, and when I view the same page, I don't get the option to merge in the pull request, although I can still comment on it if I want.

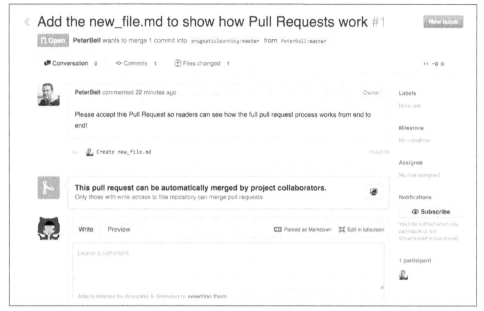

Figure 3-13. Viewing a pull request without being able to merge it

Often there will be a discussion before a pull request is merged, but we'll look at that more in Chapter 4. For now I'm just going to accept the pull request and merge it in. I can just click the "Merge pull request" button, which adds a text box where I get the option to customize the commit message for merging the pull request, as shown in Figure 3-14.

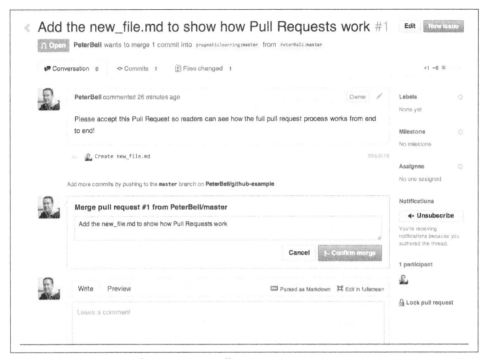

Figure 3-14. Getting ready to merge a pull request

Once I've made any changes I want to the commit message, I can just click the "Con‐firm merge" button below and to the right. The pull request is then merged, and the output is displayed, as in Figure 3-15.

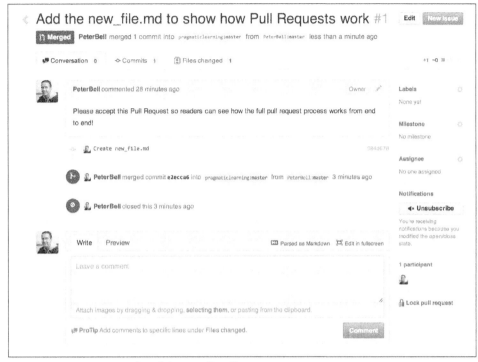

Figure 3-15. Viewing a closed (merged) pull request

Notice that we can still see the pull request message and the commit, but now we can also see who merged in the pull request and approximately when they did so. It also shows that the pull request was closed, which happens automatically when you merge it. Finally, if we look at the project page in Figure 3-16, we'll notice a couple of things.

Figure 3-16. The original (pragmaticlearning) project after merging the pull request

First, *new_file.md* has been added to the project. Second, there are *four* commits now in the original project. If we click the "4 commits" link, we can see why (see Figure 3-17).

Figure 3-17. The original project commit history

There were the two original commits in the project, there is the "Create new_file.md" commit that was made on my fork, and there is a new *merge commit* that brought the work into the original project when we merged the pull request. Whenever you merge a pull request, it will create one of these merge commits. They are really useful because the commit message (which you can edit when you merge a pull request) allows you to document *why* you decided to include the work; if you ever wanted to get rid of all of the work you merged in from a pull request, you could ask one of your developers to "revert the merge commit for that pull request" and she'd be able to easily remove all of the changes that got merged in.

Editing a File

Sometimes you might want to add a new file to a project, but most of the time you're going to want to make changes to an existing file. Let's say we wanted to edit *README.md* to let people know how to contribute to the project. Starting on the home page of your fork of the project, if you click the *README.md* filename, it'll take you to a page like Figure 3-18.

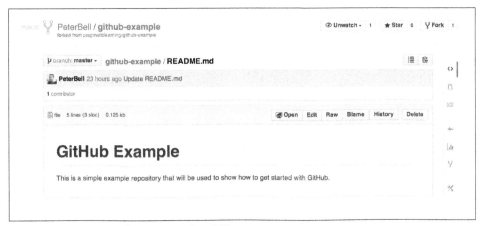

Figure 3-18. Viewing the README.md file

In Figure 3-18, you can see who last made a change to the file, how long ago the change was made, the first line of the commit message, and how many people have contributed content to the file. Above the display of the content are a number of buttons. The option we're going to use right now is the Edit button. Clicking that button takes you to the screen shown in Figure 3-19, which will allow you to change the content of the file.

Figure 3-19. Editing the README.md file

As with the screen for adding a file, once you're done with your changes, scroll down the page, enter a meaningful commit message, and click the "Commit changes" button. Once you've done that, you'll see the page displaying the *README.md* file and any additional content you added. In Figure 3-20 you can see the "how to contribute" information I just added to the file. As with the addition, if you just want to make changes to your fork, you're done. If you'd like these changes to get incorporated into the original project at *pragmaticlearning/github-example*, you'd have to create a pull request. Figure 3-20 shows the closed pull request after I created it and then merged it into the original project.

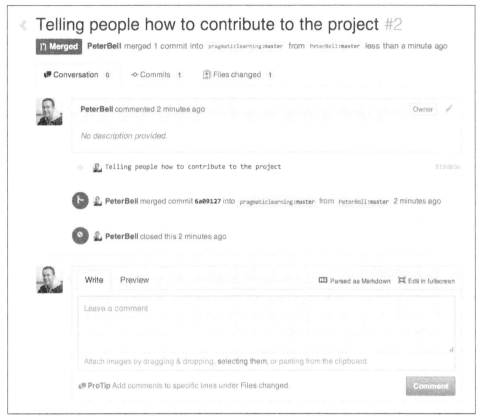

Figure 3-20. The merged pull request for the edited README.md

Renaming or Moving a File

Often you want to rename a file or move it from one folder to another. As far as Git and GitHub are concerned, both are the same process: you're changing the full name for the file, and optionally including the name of its folder. In this section, I'm going to move the *new_file.md* I created to a folder called *documentation* and I'm going to rename it *chapter_1.md*.

To start, I'm going to go to the project page for my fork of the repo, and then I'll click the *new_file.md* filename to go to the view page for *new_file.md*. Then I'll click the Edit link as I did in "Adding a File" on page 26. Doing that gets me to a screen that looks like Figure 3-21.

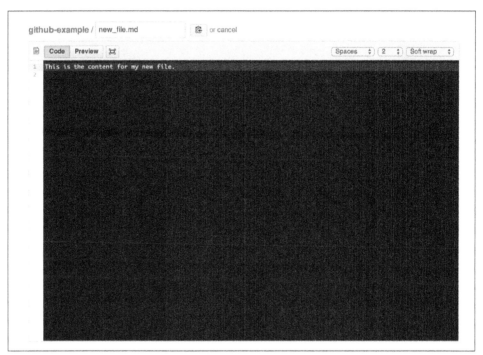

Figure 3-21. The edit screen for new_file.md

This time, instead of editing the content of the file, I'm going to go to the text box further up the page with the filename. If I just want to rename the file but keep it in the same folder, I'd just change the name of the file. If I want to put this file in another folder (whether or not it exists already), all I have to do is include a forward slash (/) in the filename. So in this case I just need to type *documentation/chapter_1.md* into the filename box. As you can see in Figure 3-22, as soon as I enter the forward slash, GitHub breaks that out as a new folder in the interface. If I wanted to move the file up a folder, I could just start by typing ../ into the filename and the file is moved up a folder.

Figure 3-22. Editing the folder or filename for a file

If you misspell the folder name, just click the cancel button shown in Figure 3-22 to start over. Once you're done with the renaming or moving of a file, scroll down the page and commit the change. Figure 3-23 shows the renamed file, now in the */documentation* folder.

Figure 3-23. The renamed file in the /documentation folder

Working with Folders

It is important to understand how Git thinks about folders—it doesn't! Git is concerned only with files. As far as it is concerned, folders are simply a place to store those files. Because of that, there is no way to add a folder to a project unless it includes at least one file.

Sometimes this is a problem. For example, in many software projects there needs to be a */build* folder where automatically generated files will be saved when compiling the software. With some systems, if you don't have such a folder, you'll be unable to use the project.

Creating a Folder

A common pattern that has emerged is to create an empty file called *.gitkeep* in any folder that you need to create but that doesn't really need to have any files. It seems a bit strange, but it works well and it is a well-understood convention, so if you ever need to create a folder, just create a *.gitkeep* file (see Figure 3-24).

Figure 3-24. A .gitkeep file to create a /build folder

Renaming a Folder

You might have guessed that just as you can't create a folder directly, you can't rename it directly either. If you want to move a single file from one folder to another, you can do that by renaming it. For example, if I wanted to move *chapter_1.md* from *documentation* to *new_docs*, I can just go to the view page for the *chapter_1.md* file, click the Edit link, and at the start of the filename box type `../` to go up a folder, followed by `new_docs` to create or put the file into that folder instead. However, there is no way you can just rename a folder on GitHub. You'd have to rename each of the files in the folder one at a time to move them to the new folder.

The Limits of Editing on GitHub

We have just run into one of the limitations of editing on GitHub. Originally GitHub was designed to allow developers to share their Git repositories with each other. Developers would make changes to their projects locally on their laptops, save those changes in Git, and then push the results to GitHub. Now that more and more non-technical people are collaborating via GitHub, it's possible to do much of your editing right on the site, but there are a number of things that you can't do via the web-based interface.

Currently, GitHub doesn't allow you to rename folders or to make any other changes to more than one file in a single commit. It also doesn't give you the power of Git to rewrite history, and it doesn't allow you to resolve conflicts online, so if there is a pull request that conflicts with another change, someone is going to have to download (clone) a copy of the repo, fix the changes, and push them back up to GitHub.

If you want to learn the basics of working with Git locally, check out the instructions in Chapter 6 for getting started with GitHub for Mac or Windows. For now, though, we're going to look at how to collaborate effectively with your team using GitHub.

CHAPTER 4

Collaboration

In this chapter we'll start by looking at how to collaborate directly on a single repository—without using forks. We'll then take some time to look more deeply into collaborating using pull requests, issues, and GitHub pages.

While forks are a good way to accept contributions from people you don't work with regularly, they are a bit too cumbersome for everyday use in a team that is working together closely. Because of this, you're probably going to want to collaborate directly on a single repository. However, it's still important to use branches and pull requests to keep your work separate.

Committing to a Branch

I've created a simple single-repo-example (*https://github.com/pragmaticlearning/ single-repo-example*) under the pragmaticlearning (*https://github.com/pragmaticlearn ing*) organization, as you can see in Figure 4-1.

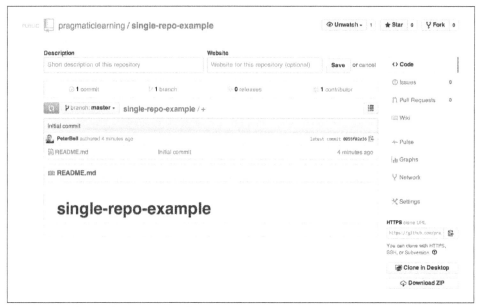

Figure 4-1. The single-repo-example repository

If I want to augment the *README.md* file, the first thing I need to do is create a branch. That way I'll be able to keep my changes separate while I'm working on them. To do that, I can just click the "branch:master" button. This creates a drop-down list with the current branches in the project and a text box for entering the name of an existing branch or the new branch that I want to create. You can see this in Figure 4-2.

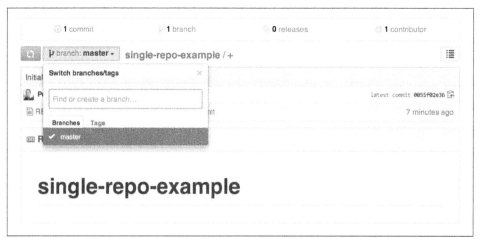

Figure 4-2. The branch drop-down list

If I create an update_readme branch, as you can see in Figure 4-3, GitHub automatically checks out that new branch. You can see this, both on the branch button where the current branch is displayed, and in the browser URL bar that ends with *tree/update_readme*, signifying that we're on the update_readme branch.

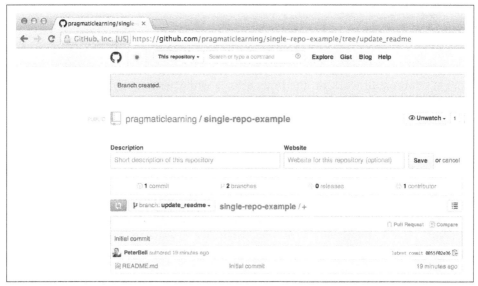

Figure 4-3. On the update_readme branch

The next step is to start to make changes. I'll edit the *README.md* file and commit the changes. As you can see in Figure 4-4, I have only one commit on the master branch, but if you look at Figure 4-5, where I've changed the branch to update_readme, in addition to the initial commit you can also see the new commit that I made on the update_readme branch.

Figure 4-4. There's still only one commit on the master branch

Figure 4-5. But there are two commits on the update_readme branch

I might continue to work on the branch for a while, getting my changes just right. Once I'm ready to get some input, I'll want to create a pull request to start a conversation about my proposed changes.

Creating a Pull Request from a Branch

To create a pull request, as in the previous chapter I'll click the Pull Request tab on the right side of the project page, and then click the green button to create a "New pull request." When I do this, as you can see in Figure 4-6, the experience is slightly different. Now GitHub isn't sure what branches I want to create a pull request between, so I have to tell it.

Figure 4-6. Starting to create a pull request from a branch

On the left you can see the base:master. That is perfect as it means that if we create a pull request, once it is accepted, it will get merged into the master branch, which is exactly what we want. However, I do need to click the "compare: master" button to tell GitHub what branch I want to create a pull request for, as you can see in

Figure 4-7. The "compare:" branch is the one that I'd like people to consider merging into master.

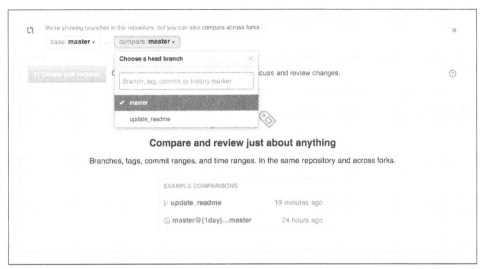

Figure 4-7. Selecting the branch for the pull request

Once I've selected a branch, the process is just the same as it was in Chapter 3 when I was creating a pull request from a fork. I click the green "Create pull request" button, enter a title and description to explain the reason for the pull request, and then click the "Create pull request" button. This creates the pull request shown in Figure 4-8.

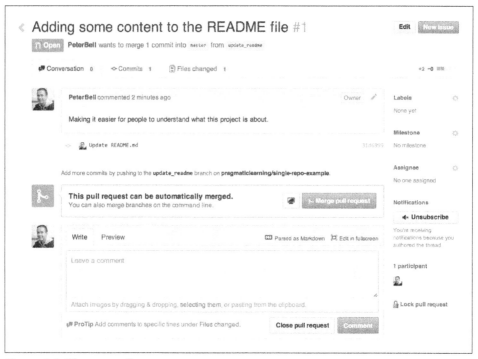

Figure 4-8. The new pull request

Collaborating on Pull Requests

Pull requests are designed to start a conversation about a proposed change—usually either a new feature or a bug fix. Originally, pull requests were created only when coding was completed to ask someone to incorporate a completed set of changes, but these days pull requests are used in a couple of different ways.

If you have a change that you're confident about, you can still create a new branch, make all your changes, and wait to create a pull request until you're done with the work. In such a case, the purpose of the pull request is just as a double-check to make sure that the rest of your team agrees with the changes you made before the changes get merged into master and pushed to production.

However, there is another way to use pull requests. In many companies, employees will often create pull requests for features that they'd like to discuss. So if you have an idea for a change but aren't sure whether it's a good idea, consider creating a branch and making the simplest possible start on the work—maybe just a small text file describing it. Once you have a commit on the branch, you can then create a pull request to kick off a discussion about the idea.

Involving People with Pull Requests

 If you've created a pull request and would like feedback from specific people on a team, @mention (pronounced "at-mention") them. To do this, within the pull request itself or a comment on the pull request, type @ and then type in the GitHub username. If the person is the owner or a collaborator on the project, the username will auto-complete.

If I wanted to get feedback from Brent Beer (a member of the GitHub training team and coauthor of this book) on some work I'd been doing, I might create a comment like "hey @brntbeer, mind looking at this PR and letting me know what you think?" The formality of the language will depend on the people you're working with, but pull request comments are often written in a fairly informal style.

Reviewing Pull Requests

If you want to see what people are working on within a project, go to the project home page, click the Pull Requests tab on the right, and you'll see a list of all of the currently open pull requests.

On most projects there should be only a few pull requests open at any one time. A good rule of thumb for a private repository is that you shouldn't usually have more than one or two open pull requests per developer. Generally, the fewer pull requests you have open, the better, as it is more valuable to keep the team focused on finishing up existing features rather than on starting new ones. The number of open pull requests on open source projects will typically be much larger, as anyone can create a pull request, and sometimes it takes a while for the core project team to review, accept, and/or close them.

When you find a pull request that you want to review, click it to view the pull request detail page.

Commenting on Pull Requests

A really important part of working with a development team is to take the time to review all of the pull requests that you might care about. Nothing is more disheartening than to work on a feature for a couple of days, create a pull request, and then get no feedback at all. Also remember that anyone *can* merge their own pull request into master, so make sure to take the time to review people's work so they aren't tempted to merge it in without at least one or two people having a look at it.

Whenever you get an email or a web notification that you've been @mentioned in a pull request, make sure to take the time to check it out ASAP and provide some useful feedback. Even if you're not named personally, take a little bit of time every day to make sure that you review any outstanding pull requests and provide your thoughts to ensure everyone is on the same page with where the project is going.

Commenting on pull requests is pretty simple. Skim down the pull request page, go to the comment box, type in your feedback, and click the Comment button.

Adding Color to Comments

Especially if you have a team that doesn't work in the same office all of the time, commenting on pull requests is often one of the more frequent ways that your team gets to interact with each other. Because of that, it's often a good idea to add a little bit of fun to the interactions.

GitHub has built-in support for emoji. Emoji are small images that are often used for displaying a mood or emotion graphically. If you look at Figure 4-9, you'll see that this comment has the :+1: (I'm in support of this feature) and the :ship: (let's merge this in and "ship" it) emoji.

Figure 4-9. A comment with some emoji

If you'd like to get a sense of some of the emoji available in GitHub, check out the Emoji Cheat Sheet (*http://www.emoji-cheat-sheet.com/*) shown in Figure 4-10.

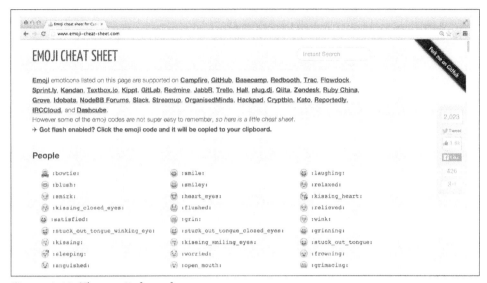

Figure 4-10. The emoji cheat sheet

Another way to add some more color to your comments on GitHub is by using animated gifs. While emoji are subtle, most animated gifs are much larger and more striking—they're often a great way to really lighten the mood or show strong support (or disapproval) for a change or a comment. To add an animated gif (or any other image) to a pull request, just drag and drop it into the comment box and it'll get uploaded automatically.

Contributing to Pull Requests

Sometimes you'll want to make a change directly to a pull request. Perhaps someone has added a new page and you'd like to fix up the marketing copy, the legal disclaimer, or even the CSS to make it display better in your favorite browser. It's easy to make a change to someone else's pull request.

The process is the same as for editing a file that we covered in the previous chapter. The only difference is that you must be on the correct branch. In this case I'm looking at the update_readme pull request for adding some content to the *README.md* file, as you can see in Figure 4-11.

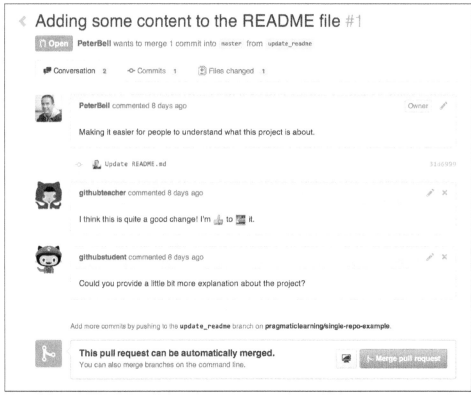

Figure 4-11. The update_readme pull request

If I decided that it would be great if the file contained a brief contributors guide, rather than just commenting that the README was missing a contributors guide, I could add one.

To make the change, all I need to do is go to the project home page and select the update_readme branch from the drop-down list of branches. I can then click the file, click Edit, and I'll get the edit screen, as you can see in Figure 4-12.

Figure 4-12. Editing README.md on the update_readme branch

I can then make my changes, scroll down the page, and enter some kind of commit message, as shown in Figure 4-13.

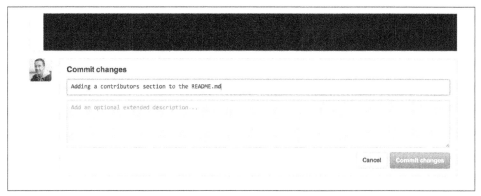

Figure 4-13. Adding a commit message

Now if I go back to the pull request page, you can see in Figure 4-14 that my commit has been added to the pull request. Anyone who is watching the pull request will get a notification that it has been updated so they can review my change and provide their feedback.

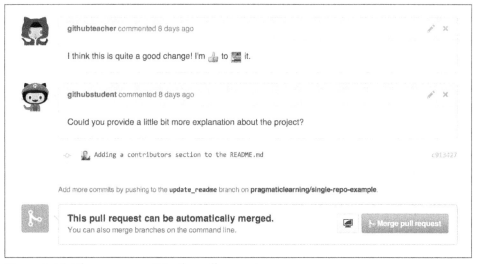

Figure 4-14. The new commit in the pull request

Testing a Pull Request

If you're a developer, before you approve a pull request that includes substantive code changes that you can't just review visually, you're going to want to download a copy of the repository (clone the repo). Then check out the branch that the pull request relates to, run the automated tests to make sure they're all passing, and then run the code and maybe do a little bit of manual testing just to make sure it seems solid. We cover cloning of repositories in Chapter 6.

If you're not a developer, you can leave this to your development team, but you do want to make sure that at least one or two people are downloading the code, running the test suite, and maybe doing a little manual testing before approving a pull request.

Merging a Pull Request

When you're ready to merge a pull request, just click the large green "Merge pull request" button, as shown in Figure 4-15.

Figure 4-15. The "Merge pull request" button

When you do so, GitHub will ask for a commit message (the default will be the title of the pull request), as shown in Figure 4-16. Once you've entered that, just click the "Confirm merge" button, and the pull request will get merged and closed, as described in Chapter 3.

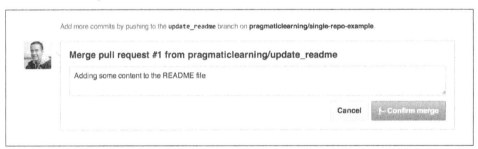

Figure 4-16. Closing a pull request

You should have some kind of policy for closing pull requests. Many teams will require one or two people other than the primary author of the pull request to provide a :+1: before a pull request is merged. Have some kind of process, but keep it lightweight. Remember, you can always revert a merge, so it's generally better to "move fast and (occasionally) break things" than have a list of 27 people who need to approve every single pull request before it can be merged.

Who Should Merge a Pull Request?

One question that often comes up is whether a pull request should be merged by the person who created the pull request or by someone else. I generally recommend that pull requests be merged by the person who created them. Here's why.

Many companies have the rule that "the person who created a pull request can't merge it." The reason for this is to make sure that someone doesn't just create a pull request and merge it in without getting any feedback. The idea is good, but I don't think the recommendation is ideal.

Most of the time, the person who created the pull request is the person who knows the most about it. As such, I always want to have that person available when her work is merged in just in case it breaks something unexpected. One of the easiest ways of making *sure* that she's around is to ask her to do the merge. So I'd recommend asking people to merge in their own pull requests, but making it clear that they shouldn't do so until they've got at least a couple of :+1:s from the rest of the team.

Pull Request Notifications

If you create a pull request, comment on one, commit to one, or are @mentioned in one, by default you'll be subscribed to the pull request. This means that whenever anyone comments on, commits to, merges, or closes the pull request, you'll be sent a notification. You can see on the right side of Figure 4-17 that I am currently subscribed to that pull request.

Figure 4-17. I'm subscribed to this pull request

If you're no longer interested in a pull request that you've been subscribed to, just click the Unsubscribe button and you'll stop receiving notifications. You will get resubscribed automatically if anyone @mentions you again in the comments. If you're *not* subscribed to a pull request that you'd like to keep an eye on, just click the Subscribe button, as shown on the right in Figure 4-18, and you will start getting notifications of any activity on that pull request.

Figure 4-18. The Subscribe button on a pull request

Best Practices for Pull Requests

There are a few best practices that are worth bearing in mind when working with pull requests:

Create pull requests for everything
Anytime you want to fix a bug or add a new feature, make sure to do it on a branch and then create a pull request to get input before merging your work into master.

Make the titles descriptive
Other team members will be looking at the pull requests page to get a sense of what's going on. The title should give them a good idea of what you're working on.

Take the time to comment
Even if you're not @mentioned. It'll give you a good sense of what's going on with the project and will improve the overall quality of the work.

@mention key people
If you want feedback from marketing, legal, and the operations team, @mention the necessary users to ensure they see the pull request and make it more likely you get feedback.

Run the tests
Make sure that at least one developer downloads the latest changes from a pull request, checks out the appropriate branch, and runs your automated tests. It isn't enough just to look at the code visually for nontrivial changes.

Have a clear policy for approving pull requests
Most companies require that one or two people other than the primary author of the pull request review and provide a :+1: before the pull request is merged in.

While pull requests are used to collaborate on work that is being done, Issues is a tool for describing bugs or new feature requests that should be discussed or worked on.

Issues

GitHub Issues provides a lightweight, easy-to-use tool for managing outstanding work—whether it's bugs that need to be fixed or new features that need to be built.

Generally, when I start a new project, I'll start by managing both bugs and features using GitHub Issues, and I'll move to another tool like Pivotal tracker, JIRA, Light-House, Trello, or Asana only if I need features that Issues doesn't provide.

Creating a New Issue

To create a new issue, click the Issues tab and then click the "New issue" button, shown in Figure 4-19.

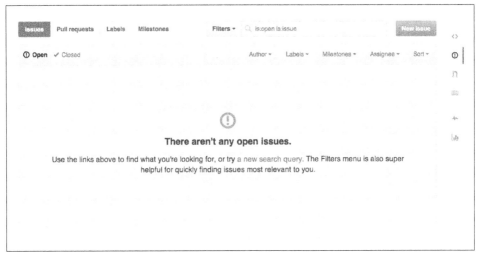

Figure 4-19. The "New issue" button

When you click the "New issue" button, you'll see a form similar to Figure 4-20 for entering the details of the issue you want to document.

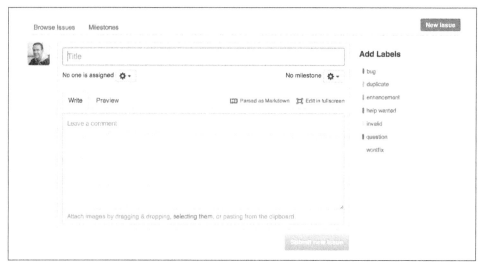

Figure 4-20. The "New issue" form

Enter a descriptive title that will quickly give people a sense of the bug or feature you want to describe. If you know who should be working on the issue, you can select that person from a drop-down list of contributors by clicking the button to the right of the "No one is assigned" text label. To the right of that label, you can also select a milestone if you're assigning issues to sprints or other deadlines, and then enter a more comprehensive description below in the comment field. On the right you'll notice a list of labels. Select all of the labels that apply, and then click the green "Submit new issue" button at the bottom of the page to create the issue.

Managing Milestones for Issues

The milestones feature of Issues is often used to assign issues to a particular sprint or an external deadline like "July 29th investor presentation." To add a new milestone, click the Issues tab on the right side of the page. Then click the Milestones button in the upper-left portion of the screen next to "Issues," "Pull requests," and "Labels." You'll see the view look very similar to issues and pull requests, and on the right you'll see a button to create a "New milestone," as you can see in Figure 4-21.

Figure 4-21. The "New milestone" button

Click the "New milestone" button and you'll see a form similar to Figure 4-22 asking you for a title, an optional description, and an optional due date.

Figure 4-22. Adding a new milestone

Enter at least a title and click the "Create milestone" button at the bottom right of the page; you'll see the new milestone added to your list of milestones, as shown in Figure 4-23. You can now edit the milestone, close it, delete it, or browse a list of the issues associated with the milestone.

Figure 4-23. The new milestone

Managing Labels for Issues

You'll probably also want to create some custom labels for your project. Click the Labels button in the upper-left portion of the screen next to "Issues," "Pull requests," and "Milestones." From this page, shown in Figure 4-24, we'll be able to edit titles and colors, and delete and create new labels.

Figure 4-24. The Labels page

To delete a label, click Delete on the right side of that label's row. To edit a label, click Edit; it will change to allow you to edit both the text and the color for the label, as shown in Figure 4-25.

Figure 4-25. Editing a label

If you want to add a new label, click the "New label" button and you'll see a text box, a set of colors to choose from, and a "Create label" button, as shown in Figure 4-26.

Figure 4-26. Adding a new label

Commenting on Issues

As with pull requests:

- To comment on an issue, just click the issue, scroll down to the comment box, enter your comment, and click the Comment button.
- Make sure to take a little time every day to see if there are any new issues, and respond to any @mentions ASAP.
- Feel free to use emoji and animated gifs to add a little fun to the process of collaboration.

Referencing Issues in a Commit

If you make a commit that either relates to or fixes an issue, just include a pound sign (#) followed by the number of the issue somewhere in the commit message, and the commit will show up in the history for that issue. Prefix the issue number with a word like "closes," "fixes," or "resolves" if the commit solves the issue, and when that commit is merged into your default branch (usually master), the issue will be closed automatically!

Best Practices for Issues

Here are some best practices to consider when thinking about how best to use GitHub issues:

Create "Bug" and "Feature" labels
> To make it easy to just see outstanding bugs or features.

Use milestones if they fit your workflow
> If you have either external deadlines or an internal cadence based around something like sprints, feel free to use milestones to assign issues to delivery dates. If you don't use date-based deliveries, consider using milestones (without dates) to group like pieces of work. For example, you could have a milestone for "Complete site redesign" and another one for "Launch e-commerce features."

Be careful when assigning issues
> Generally, it's better for members of your development team to "pull" the work they're interested in rather than for you to "push" a bunch of work for them to do.

Make extensive use of labels
> In addition to high-level labels to distinguish "Bugs" and "Features," you can use labels for a range of other purposes. Consider adding labels to track the status of work, to assign the work to different groups ("iOS," "server side," "frontend," etc.), and even for tracking other interesting information like the severity of a bug or the business objective that the new feature is designed to support.

Wikis

At some point in the life of your project, your *README.md* file will start to get too long to be usable. At that point (if not before), you should consider using the wiki feature in GitHub.

A wiki is a very simple content management system that makes it easy for a group of collaborators to build a set of interlinked pages. Typically, GitHub wikis are used for capturing end-user documentation, developer documentation, or both so that all of the information relating to a project is accessible through the project's GitHub page.

Getting Started with a Wiki

If your project doesn't yet have a wiki, start by going to Settings and scrolling down to the Features area, as shown in Figure 4-27. Make sure that the Wikis checkbox is selected. This is also a chance to check the next box if you're going to be creating a public project and want to limit it so that only collaborators on the project are able to update the documentation on the wiki.

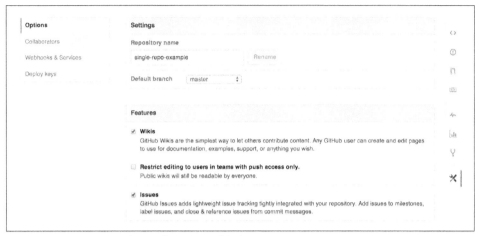

Figure 4-27. Ensuring that wikis are enabled

Once you've ensured that you have wikis enabled, click the Wiki tab on the right side of any page, and if you haven't yet added any content, you'll see a page like Figure 4-28.

Figure 4-28. The default wiki page

Click the green "Create the first page" button, and you'll see a page similar to Figure 4-29.

Figure 4-29. Creating your first wiki page

By default the first page is called "home," although you can change this by editing the title. Then you can enter your content in the text area. You'll notice that there are a number of buttons above the text area for styling, but this is deliberately not a full, in-place WYSIWYG (what-you-see-is-what-you-get) editor. Instead, the buttons will just insert the appropriate markdown into the text area. If you want to see what it'll look like, click the Preview tab above the formatting buttons and you'll see the markdown rendered, as shown in Figure 4-30.

Figure 4-30. Previewing your new wiki page

If you click the "Edit mode" drop-down list, you get the option of changing to a range of different selected formatting syntaxes, as you can see in Figure 4-31. However, I'd recommend using markdown as it's the same format used by the GitHub team and is used in other areas within GitHub, such as issues and pull request comments.

Figure 4-31. Alternative editing formats

When you're done with the content, enter a short (optional) description in the "Edit message" text box to describe why you made the change, and click the "Save page" button.

Adding and Linking to a Page on Your Wiki

Anytime you want to add a new page to your wiki, just click the "New page" button at the top right of any wiki page and it'll allow you to add a page to the site. Once you've added the page, it will appear in the Pages section to the right of the screen, as you can see in Figure 4-32.

Figure 4-32. The Pages list in a wiki

To add a link to a new page from an existing page, start by using the Pages list to navigate to the page you want to add a link *to*. Then copy the URL from your browser for that page to the clipboard—we'll need that in a moment. Next, use the Pages list to navigate to the page you want to add the link *on*. Click the Edit button at the top of that page to the right. Go to the place in the content are a where you want to add the link and click the link button in the top bar (it looks like two circles linked together). Clicking it pops up a dialog box, as shown in Figure 4-33.

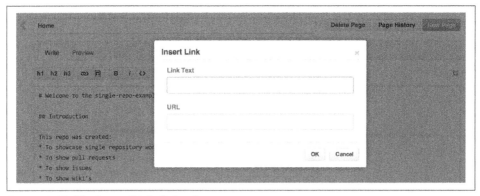

Figure 4-33. The Insert Link dialog box

In the first box, type whatever you want the link text to be—ideally something that describes the page it's linking to. Then in the URL text box, paste the URL of the wiki page you want to link to from your clipboard.

If you'd really like to make the most of your wiki (or issues or pull request comments), make sure to check out this page that provides a really good introduction to GitHub flavored markdown (*https://github.github.com/github-flavored-markdown/*).

GitHub Pages

Wikis are a great tool for creating documentation on GitHub, and because they live right next to the code, they're much more likely to be kept updated than a separate document. However, sometimes you want to create a more customized website to share information about yourself, your organization, or your project. That's where GitHub pages come in. GitHub pages is a feature that allows you to create and host web pages right on GitHub.

Creating a Website for Your Project

Whenever you create a repository on GitHub, you have the option of adding GitHub pages to provide a web page for promoting or describing the project. To get started with GitHub pages, click Settings, scroll down to the GitHub Pages area, and click the "Automatic page generator" button. You'll see a screen similar to Figure 4-34.

Figure 4-34. The GitHub pages form

The form allows you to enter a project name, a tagline, a body where you can create a first cut of the content for the page using markdown, and if you want, there is an option to add a tracking ID to record traffic information using Google Analytics. Once you're done with the first page, click the "Continue to layouts" button, which takes you to a page similar to Figure 4-35, where you can pick from a range of pre-designed themes to get started with.

Figure 4-35. Selecting a layout for your GitHub pages site

When you're happy with the look and feel, click Publish page toward the top right of the page, and your website will be created. You can view the website at *http://organization_name.github.io/projectname*. For example, I just created a web page for a project called github-example that is under the pragmaticlearning organization, and the page is available at *http://pragmaticlearning.github.io/github-example*.

Under the hood, when you create a GitHub page for a project, it adds a new gh-pages branch to your project. Select that branch from the drop-down list and you'll see a screen similar to Figure 4-36, which shows the generated website code that you can customize if you're comfortable working with HTML and CSS.

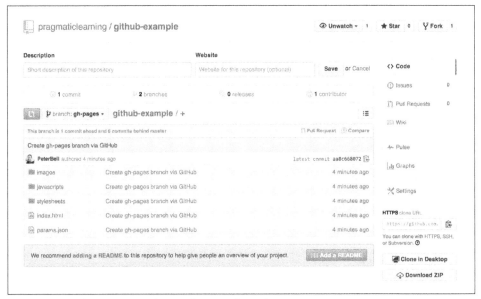

Figure 4-36. The contents of your gh-pages branch

Creating a Website for Yourself or Your Organization

If you want to create a website for yourself or your organization using GitHub pages, you need to create a project named username.github.io. For personal and organizational GitHub pages, instead of having a gh-pages branch, the contents of your master branch are used to build your website.

If you want to create a website for your organization, go to the organization home page and click the "+ New repository" button. Make sure to make the repository name "organization_name.github.io," and then check the "Initialize this repository with a README" checkbox, as shown in Figure 4-37.

Figure 4-37. Creating a GitHub pages repo for an organization

If you create such a project, click the Settings link, and scroll down to the GitHub Pages section, you'll see that it shows that you've already been published as a GitHub Pages website (see Figure 4-38).

Figure 4-38. The settings tab for a GitHub pages organization site

If you know HTML and CSS, you can just build your website here. If you want to take advantage of the built-in generator, you can overwrite the project by clicking the Automatic page generator button, which will work just as it did for the project GitHub pages websites.

CHAPTER 5

Creating and Configuring

So far we've looked at how to view, edit, and collaborate on projects. In this chapter we're going to go through the process of creating and configuring a GitHub repository for a new project.

If you're working with developers on a contract basis, you'll want to create the repository they use to work on. By creating the repo, it means that you'll always have access to the code and the additional information contained in pull requests, issues, and wikis. Once you've created the repo, you can then add the developers as collaborators so they'll have access to the project—until you decide to revoke it. You do *not* want contract developers to create the repo for you. If they do, they'll be able to remove *you* from the project at any time.

Creating a Repository

To create a new project on GitHub, click the + sign to the right of your username at the top right of the page. Then click the "New repository" option in the drop-down list. You'll see the new repository form, as shown in Figure 5-1.

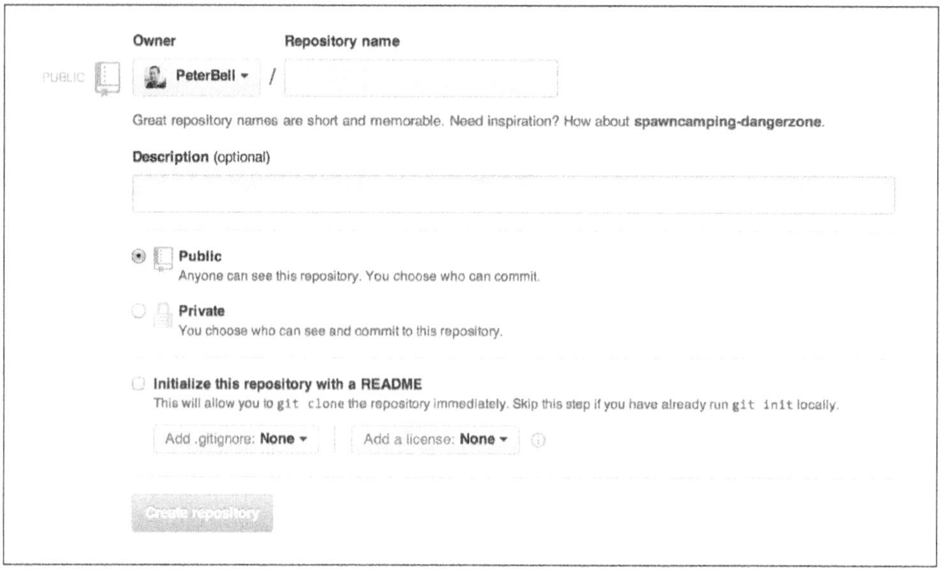

Figure 5-1. The new repository form

The first thing to do is decide whether to create the repository under your username or under an organization. You can see in Figure 5-2 a list of the possible organizations to which I could add a new repository. If you don't have access to any organizations, you'll just leave this defaulted to your username. Remember, you'll always be able to transfer the project later if you want to.

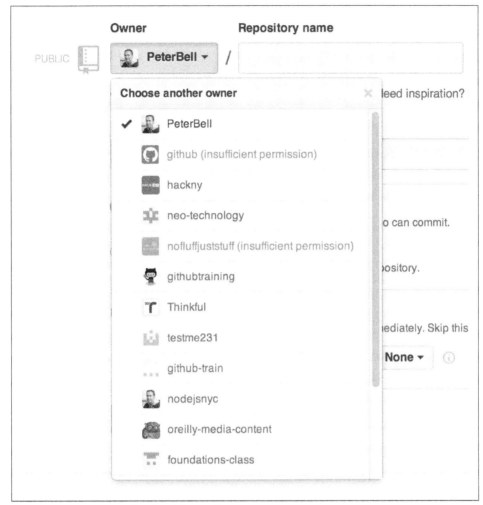

Figure 5-2. Selecting who should own the new repository

The next step is to give the repository a name. Names should be comprised of letters, numbers, hyphens, and/or underscores. Any other characters will be replaced with a hyphen.

After entering the name, you need to decide whether to make the repository private or not. Public repositories can be viewed by anyone. Private repositories can be viewed only by people that you specifically invite as collaborators. In either case, the project can be modified only by people you add as collaborators.

Generally, if your code is commercially sensitive, you'll pay the few dollars a month to be able to keep it private. If it isn't, you can just create a public repository, and it won't cost you a thing. If you don't see the option to make the repository private, you'll need to upgrade the user or organization you're creating the project under to allow it to host private repositories.

The final decision you'll need to make when creating a new repository is whether or not to initialize it with a *README* file by checking the checkbox, as shown in Figure 5-3.

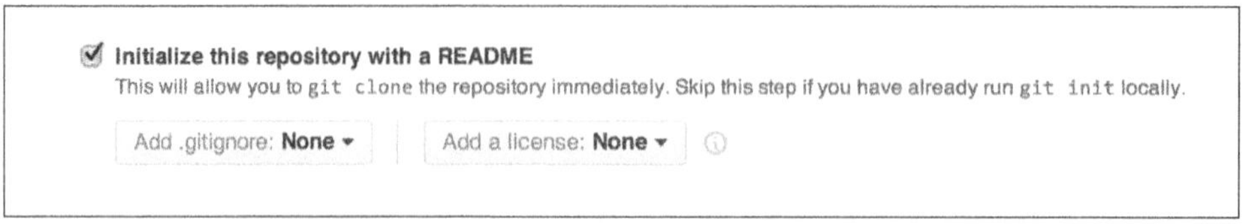

Figure 5-3. Initializing a repository with a README.md

Most developers will not check the box to initialize the repo. They'll just create a project locally, save it using Git, and then push their work up to GitHub. However, if you're not a developer, you'll probably want to initialize the project with a *README* as it allows you to create a project without having to create a local Git repository and upload it. Then your developers will be able to clone (download) the repo and add all of their code. Once you're ready, click the Create repository button, and the new repo will be created.

If you initialize the repo with a *README*, it will create a project and take you to a screen that looks something like Figure 5-4. That project is ready for your developers to clone and start committing to.

Figure 5-4. A new project initialized with a README.md

If you *don't* initialize your repo, you'll see a screen like Figure 5-5. Notice that you or someone on your team is going to have to upload an existing Git repository before anyone will be able to clone or work with this repository.

Figure 5-5. A new project that needs a repository to be uploaded

Adding Collaborators

Once you've created and initialized your repository, the next step is to add any collaborators. If you've created a public repository, you may not need to add collaborators, especially if you're just working with people occasionally. Ask them to fork your repo and send you a pull request any time they have a contribution to make. However, if you created a private repo or you have people who will be working on the project regularly, you should add them as collaborators.

If you've added the repository to an organization, you can manage access using teams, which we'll look at later in this chapter. However, if you just added the repo to your personal account, you'll have to add collaborators individually.

To add collaborators, click the Settings link in the bottom-right corner of the screen and then click the Collaborators tab, as shown in Figure 5-6. You may be asked for your password just to confirm that it's you making the change.

Figure 5-6. The Settings link and the Collaborators tab

To add collaborators, you'll need to know the GitHub usernames of the people you want to work with. Start typing a username, and the name will auto-complete, as shown in Figure 5-7. Select the auto-completed name and then click the "Add collaborator" button.

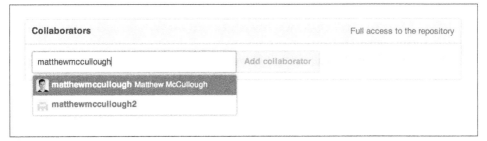

Figure 5-7. Auto-completion of a collaborator

Once you've added collaborators, it's worth taking a little bit of time to go through the other configuration options to see if there's anything else you want to set up.

Configuring a Repository

To configure a repository, start by clicking the Settings link at the bottom right of the page. By default you'll go to the Options tab within Settings, as shown in Figure 5-8, which allows you to configure some high-level settings.

Figure 5-8. The Settings→Options screen

The first option is to rename the repository. If you change the repo name in the text box, the Rename button will become active, allowing you to change the name of the project. Don't worry if your developers are already connected to the project. They won't have to change anything—anybody using the old name or URL to access the project will be redirected automatically.

You also get the option to change the "Default branch" from master to any other branch. Generally it's best to leave this option alone, but if your development team really wanted to create a new default branch, they could do so and you could make it the default branch here. The default branch is used for features like auto-closing of issues. Usually, when you have a commit message that says something like "closes #10" or "fixed #10," when that commit is merged into the master branch, it will automatically close issue #10. However, it's really when the commit gets merged into the default branch, so if you wanted to have a default branch named "trunk" or something else, you could do that if you really wanted to.

On the Settings→Options screen, you also get the chance to configure wikis and issues. By default, new projects have both wikis and issues enabled. Just uncheck the boxes to disable them. If you want to limit the wiki on a public project so that only collaborators can edit the content, check the necessary box.

As you go further down the Settings→Options screen, you'll see some additional configuration settings, as shown in Figure 5-9.

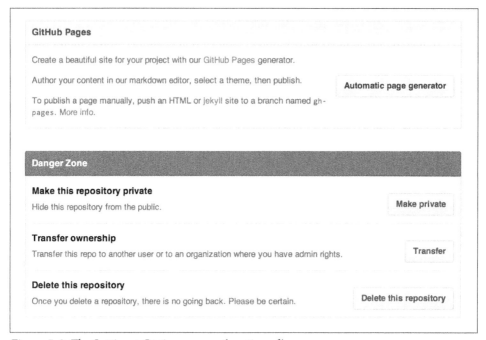

Figure 5-9. The Settings→Options screen (continued)

If you'd like to add a website to the project, click "Automatic page generator" in the GitHub Pages area to configure that.

Finally, we come to the "Danger Zone." It allows you to change the accessibility of a project between private and public. It also gives you the option to transfer the ownership of the project to another user or organization and, if you really want, it allows you to delete the repository. Don't worry about hitting the Delete button accidentally.

If you click the Delete button, you'll be asked to confirm that you really want to do that, as shown in Figure 5-10.

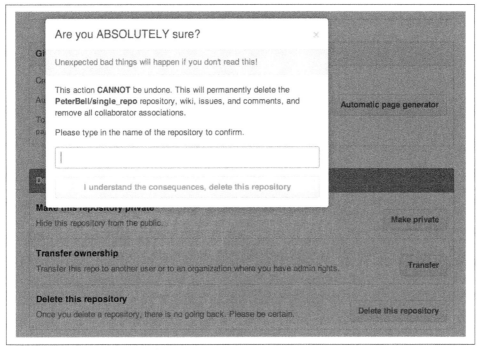

Figure 5-10. The Delete confirmation pop-up

Integrating with Other Systems

Sometimes you'll want to connect GitHub to other pieces of software that you use—anything from continuous integration servers that regularly run automated tests, to project management or bug tracking software. There are three ways of connecting software to a GitHub repository.

One option is the GitHub API. Go to *http://developer.github.com*, as shown in Figure 5-11, and click the API link at the top of the page to learn how to use the GitHub API to do pretty much anything with a repository automatically.

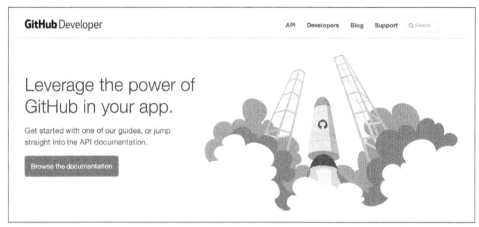

Figure 5-11. The GitHub developer page

The API allows your developers to query and change almost anything they want with a repository, but sometimes they'll want to just be notified when a specific action occurs. For example, they might want their program to get notified every time someone adds a new issue or pushes work up to GitHub. If they want to have notifications automatically sent to their project, they should be using the Webhooks option that can be configured by going to Settings → Webhooks & Services, as shown in Figure 5-12.

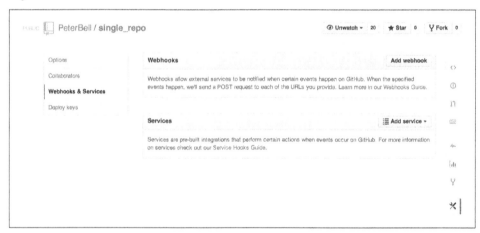

Figure 5-12. The Webhooks & Services page

Clicking the Add webhook button toward the top-right corner of the screen takes you to the "Add webhook" screen, as shown in Figure 5-13.

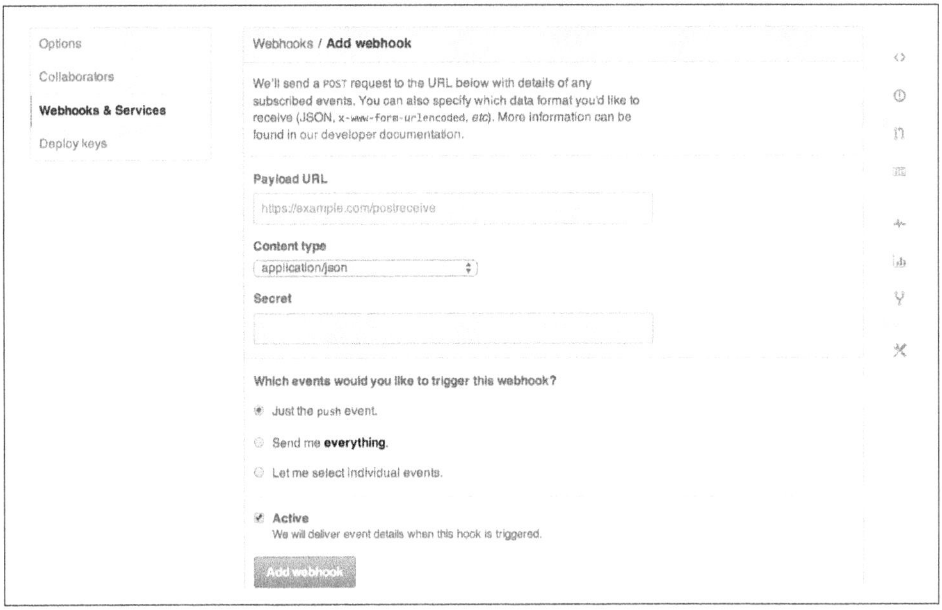

Figure 5-13. The "Add webhook" screen

This screen allows you to tell GitHub to send a notification to your custom software every time a particular type of event occurs. You need to provide the URL that your software will be listening on, the kind of content you want delivered, an optional secret (so that not just anyone can send fake information to that URL), and what kinds of events you'd like to have the software be notified about. If your developers are implementing a custom integration, they'll run you through exactly how they'd like to have the webhook(s) configured.

The final integration option is one that doesn't require developers. Go to Settings → Webhooks & Services, and click the "Add service" link. A drop-down list will appear, similar to Figure 5-14.

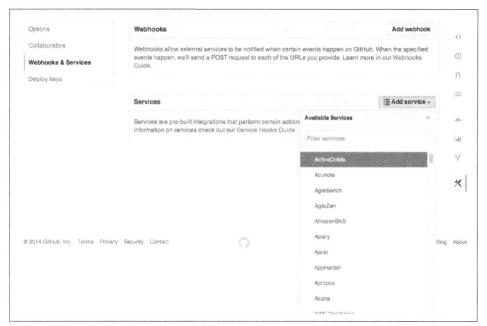

Figure 5-14. The "Add service" drop-down list

If you're using popular software with a prewritten integration, start typing the name of the software into the "Filter services" text box and fairly quickly you should see the name of the software. Click the name to display a screen that tells you what you need to do to integrate with that software.

For example, let's say you wanted to integrate with Basecamp. Start typing "Base-camp," select Basecamp from the list, and you'll see a screen like Figure 5-15 asking you to enter the URL of your Basecamp project and the credentials that you want Git-Hub to use to log in.

Figure 5-15. Integrating GitHub with Basecamp

Each integration is different—both in terms of what information you need to provide to connect to the third-party software and in terms of the functionality provided by the integration. As you can see in Figure 5-16, the install notes for integrating with Asana are quite different than those for integrating with Basecamp.

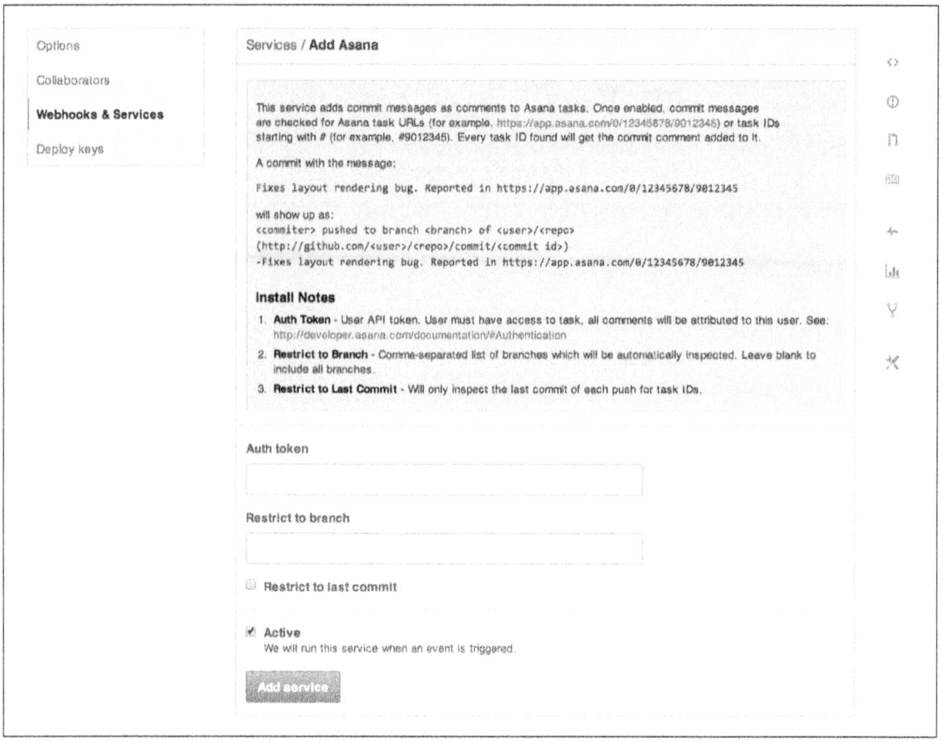

Figure 5-16. Integrating GitHub with Asana

"Deploy keys" is the last tab in the Settings section for a GitHub repository. Clicking the link displays a page similar to Figure 5-17.

Figure 5-17. Configuring deploy keys

In addition to other people needing access to your repository, sometimes you'll want to provide the ability for other software to connect to it. For example, your development team will probably create an automated build system that will allow them to just click a button to deploy the latest changes from GitHub to your production server.

If they do that, the build system will need the ability to access the repository. There are a number of ways of providing that access. One option is to create a *machine account*. This is where you create a new GitHub user just for your build machine and add that user as a collaborator. That's a particularly good approach if your build system needs access to a number of different repositories.

Another option is just to create a *deploy key*. A deploy key is an SSH key (a Secure Shell key) that is created to allow a particular piece of software to access a single repository on GitHub. Don't worry about this too much, but if your development team asks you to set up a deploy key, just ask them to email you the public SSH key and to give you a name for the key (e.g., "build server"), and then you can use that information to fill out the "Add deploy key" screen, as shown in Figure 5-18.

Figure 5-18. Adding a deploy key to a GitHub repo

Personal Versus Organizational

When you create a repository, the first question you need to answer is whether you should add the repository to your personal user account or whether you should add it to an organization instead.

If you are creating a personal project (whether for free or for profit), you probably want to just create it under your personal GitHub account. However, if you're creating a project that you know you will want to be owned and/or managed by an entity other than yourself—whether a not-for-profit or a corporation—you should probably create an organization first and then create the project under the organization so you can easily transfer ownership of the project over time.

This isn't the most important decision. You can always transfer the ownership of a repository, so if in doubt, feel free to just create the repo under your user account. However, if you *know* that you're going to be building a project for an organization, you might want to create the organization first.

Creating an Organization

To create an organization, log in to GitHub, click the + sign to the right of your username at the top right of the page, and from the drop-down list shown in Figure 5-19, click the "New organization" option.

Figure 5-19. The first step in adding a new organization

Clicking the link will take you to a page similar to Figure 5-20 that will allow you to create a new organization.

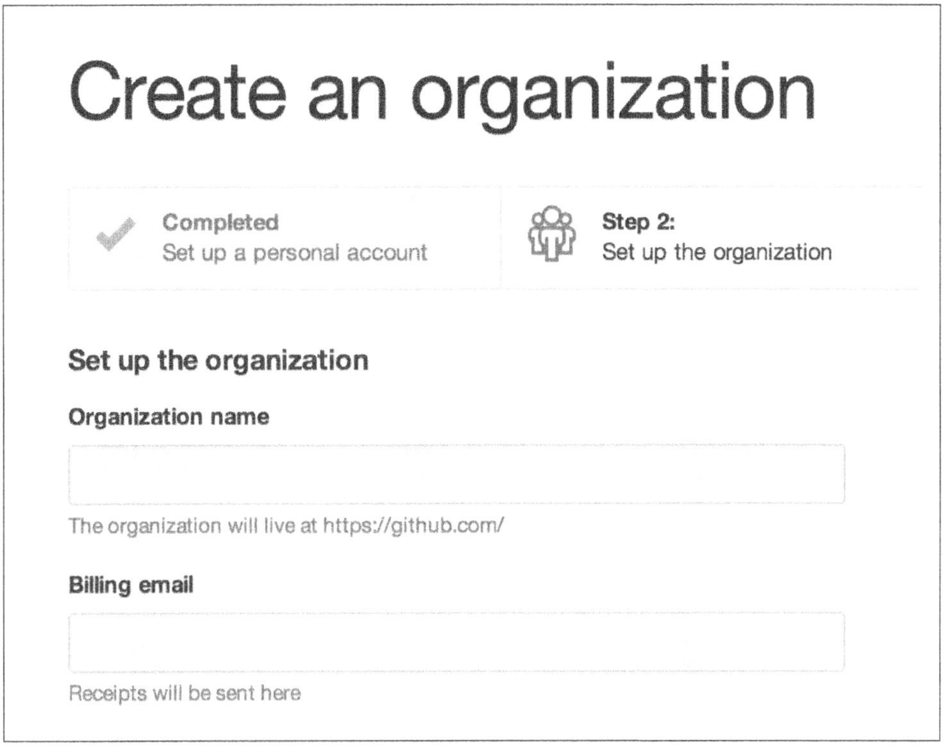

Create an organization

✓	**Completed** Set up a personal account	🏛	**Step 2:** Set up the organization

Set up the organization

Organization name

[   ]

The organization will live at https://github.com/

Billing email

[   ]

Receipts will be sent here

Figure 5-20. Creating a new organization

Start by giving the organization a name and entering the email address for the billing contact. You'll then want to select a plan. If all of your projects are openly accessible, you can create an open source organization for free. If you want to host private repositories, you'll need at least a bronze plan that will allow you to host up to 10 private repositories (and unlimited public repositories) for $25 a month.

If you choose to create an organization that can host private repositories, you'll be asked for either credit card or PayPal information to make the monthly payments.

Once you've created an organization, the next thing you'll want to do is set up some teams.

Managing Teams

If you create a repository under your user account, you can just add collaborators directly to a project. However, if you create a repository under an organization and you want to allow other people to access it, you'll have to create teams.

By default, when you create an organization, GitHub will create a team called "Owners" and you'll be assigned to that team. If you want to allow other people access to the project, you'll have to either add them to the Owners team for the organization or you'll need to create a new team.

Most of the time you'll want to create a new team with limited permissions. I'll often create a team called "Collaborators" for people I want to work with on a project. If I'm within a larger organization, I might also create teams for business units or functions like marketing and legal.

To create a team, go to the organization home page and click the Teams link on the right side of the page, as shown in Figure 5-21.

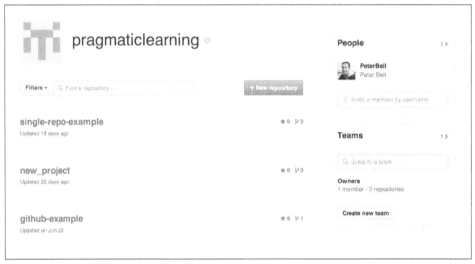

Figure 5-21. The organization home page

When you get to the Teams page, you should see a screen similar to Figure 5-22. It will show a list of all of the teams within your organization and a list of icons showing the members of each team.

Figure 5-22. Viewing the teams within your organization

To create a new team, click the green "+ New Team" button at the top right of the content area. You'll see a screen similar to Figure 5-23.

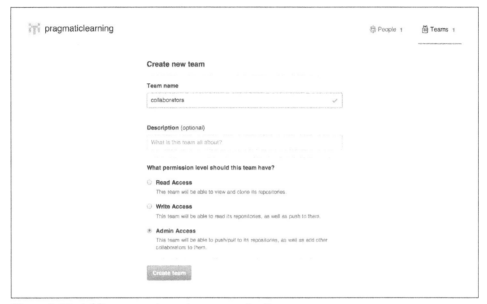

Figure 5-23. Adding a new team to an organization

Give your team a name. If you're just working with a couple of developers on a single product, it might be something as simple as a "Collaborators." If you are part of a larger organization, the name could be the business function or even the name of the project team: "mobile devs," "API team," etc.

You can add an optional description if the intent of the team wouldn't be obvious to members of your organization, and then provide the team with read, write, or admin access. If you provide read access, they'll be able to only view, clone, and use the software. If you provide write access, they'll also be able to push to the repo. If you provide them with admin access, they'll also be able to add additional collaborators to the projects to which they have access. Then click the "Create team" button.

Once you've created a team, the next step is to add members to the team. As shown in Figure 5-24, just start to enter the GitHub username for each person you want to add to the team, and the name will auto-complete.

Figure 5-24. Adding a new user to a team

If you ever need to remove someone from a team, just click the team and then click the Remove button to the right of the username you want to delete. If you need to delete a team, on the Teams page, click the team you want to delete and you'll see a screen similar to Figure 5-25.

Figure 5-25. The team detail page

Click the Settings button on the left side of the screen and you'll see a screen similar to Figure 5-26.

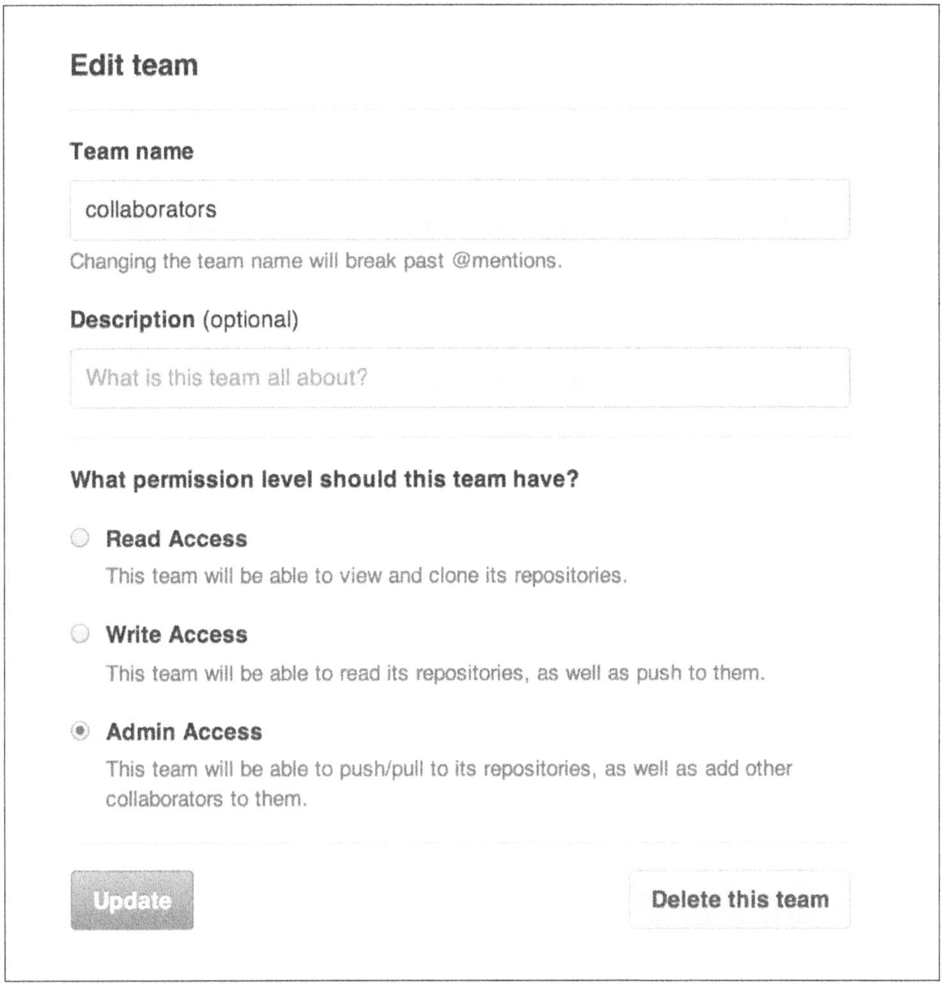

Edit team

Team name

collaborators

Changing the team name will break past @mentions.

Description (optional)

What is this team all about?

What permission level should this team have?

○ **Read Access**

This team will be able to view and clone its repositories.

○ **Write Access**

This team will be able to read its repositories, as well as push to them.

◉ **Admin Access**

This team will be able to push/pull to its repositories, as well as add other collaborators to them.

Update   **Delete this team**

Figure 5-26. The team settings page

If you want to delete the team, click the "Delete this team" button at the bottom of the page. You'll be asked whether you're sure. Just click OK, and the team will be deleted.

Congratulations! If you've gotten this far in the book, you should be ready to do almost anything with a GitHub repo. You should be able to view the state of a project, edit the files in a project, collaborate with your team, and create and configure a new repository. In the next chapter, we're going to look at how you can use the GitHub for Windows or GitHub for Mac desktop client to download a copy of a GitHub repository and to make some simple changes to it on your laptop.

CHAPTER 6

Downloading

You may never need to clone (download) a copy of a repository at all. As we've seen in this book, you can use the GitHub web interface to view the state of a project, edit content, collaborate with your team, and set up and configure a repository. However, sometimes it's necessary to clone a repository. In this chapter we look at why you might want to clone a repo and how you would do so using either GitHub for Mac or GitHub for Windows. If you're running Linux, you'll probably be better off just installing Git directly and learning the command-line interface for working with Git repositories, but that's outside of the scope of this book.

Why Clone a Repository?

There are a number of reasons why you might decide to clone a repository. Some of the most common ones include the following:

Creating a backup
When you clone a repository, it creates a full copy of the project—including all branches, tags, and history—on your computer. Sometimes it's worth cloning a repository and pulling the changes down regularly just to know that you have a full copy of the project safely on your machine.

Editing in an IDE
The web-based interface isn't as powerful as editing in an IDE (Integrated Development Environment) or your favorite text editor, so if you're editing content all day, you're going to want to do that locally on your machine.

Editing offline
You can't edit directly on GitHub unless you have an Internet connection, so if you want to be able to keep working on your project whether or not you're connected, you're going to want to clone your repo and work on it locally.

Editing multiple files
> One of the key limitations when editing on GitHub directly is that there is no way to group a set of related changes and make them as a single commit.

Running the code
> Sometimes you'll want to be able to run the code locally to test exactly how it works.

Running the tests
> If you have automated tests for a project, it's also good to be able to run those tests locally to confirm that recent changes haven't broken the software.

If you need to do any of the preceding things, you'll need to either install the Git version control system directly onto your computer or you'll need to install a GUI (graphical user interface) that makes it easier for you to use Git to perform common operations.

A number of different applications are available that provide a GUI for working with your Git repositories. In this chapter, we're going to cover the GUIs provided by Git-Hub: GitHub for Mac and GitHub for Windows.

GitHub for Mac

To get a copy of GitHub for Mac, start by going to *https://mac.github.com/*. You should see a screen similar to Figure 6-1.

Figure 6-1. The GitHub Mac web page

Click the "Download GitHub for Mac" link to download a ZIP file to the folder that your browser downloads files to—usually that will be your *Downloads* folder. Double-click the ZIP file, and it should expand to a file called *GitHub.app* in the same folder, as shown in Figure 6-2.

Figure 6-2. The GitHub for Mac ZIP file and application file

Drag the *GitHub.app* file into your *Applications* folder. Then click the *Applications* folder, and double-click the *GitHub.app* file. You might see a security warning to let you know that *GitHub.app* is an application downloaded from the Internet, as shown in Figure 6-3. That's fine—just click the Open button in that dialog box, and the Git-Hub application will start.

Figure 6-3. The warning that you're running a program downloaded from the Internet

You should see a screen similar to Figure 6-4 thanking you for trying GitHub for Mac.

Figure 6-4. The setup wizard for GitHub for Mac

Click Continue, enter your login and password for GitHub, and click the "Sign in" button. If you have enabled two-factor authentication to make your account more secure, you'll be asked to enter the code that was texted to your mobile phone.

Once you've done this, you should see a screen similar to Figure 6-5.

Figure 6-5. Confirming your user account in GitHub for Mac

Click the Continue button again, and you'll be prompted for some information to configure Git. In the first text box, enter the name you want to be known by, and in the second, enter the email address you'd like your commits to be associated with. Usually you'll enter your full name into the first text box and the same email address you use for your GitHub account in the second one, as I've done in Figure 6-6.

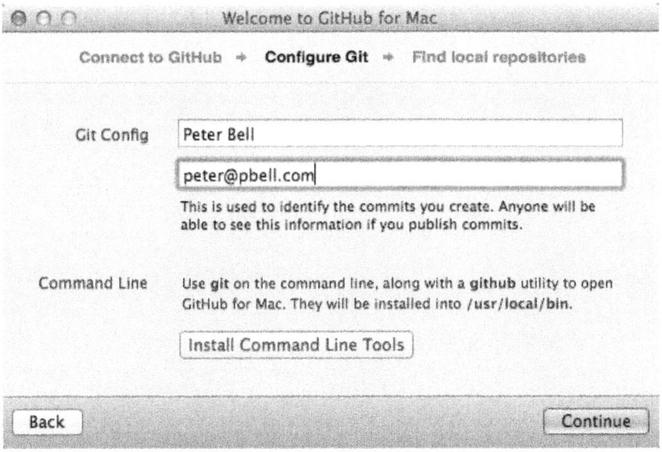

Figure 6-6. Configuring your Git settings

Just below the text boxes is a section called Command Line. Click the Install Command Line Tools button. By installing these tools, if you *do* ever want to use Git on the command line, you'll be able to. You will have to enter your system's administrative credentials. When you're done, you should see a screen similar to Figure 6-7 showing that the installation is complete and the command-line tools have been installed successfully.

Figure 6-7. The command-line tools have been installed successfully

Click the OK button and then the Continue button and you'll be taken to a screen that allows you to find local repositories. For now, just click the Done button and you'll go to the home screen in GitHub for Mac that looks like Figure 6-8.

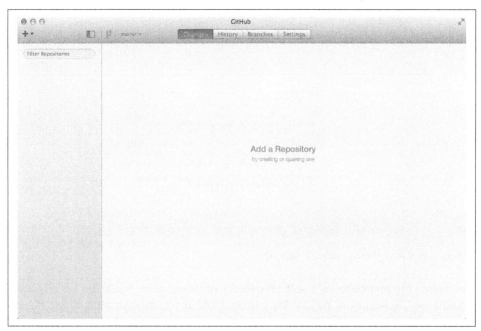

Figure 6-8. The home screen in GitHub for Mac

Once you've configured GitHub for Mac, don't worry if you get an email similar to the one shown in Figure 6-9 letting you know that "A new public key was added to your account." This is just GitHub letting you know that you've successfully connected GitHub for Mac to your GitHub account. It does that by adding a new public key that will allow GitHub for Mac to connect to your GitHub account.

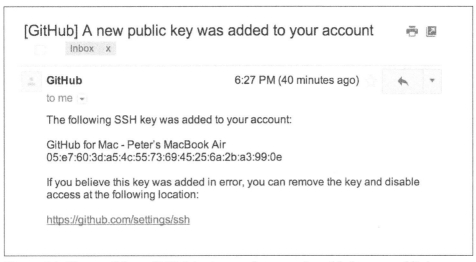

Figure 6-9. The email from GitHub letting you know you've added a new public key

Now that you've installed GitHub for Mac, go to a repository that you'd like to clone (download) and that you own or are a collaborator on. You can clone any public repo, but you won't be able to push your changes back up to GitHub unless you're either an owner or a collaborator. If you look at the bottom-right corner of the page, you should see the "Clone in Desktop" button, as shown at the bottom right of Figure 6-10.

Figure 6-10. A repo with the "Clone in Desktop" button

Click the "Clone in Desktop" button. The exact result when you click the button will depend on the browser and version that you're running. In Chrome, I get the pop-up in Figure 6-11 asking whether I should let the browser talk to *GitHub.app*. You should get something similar.

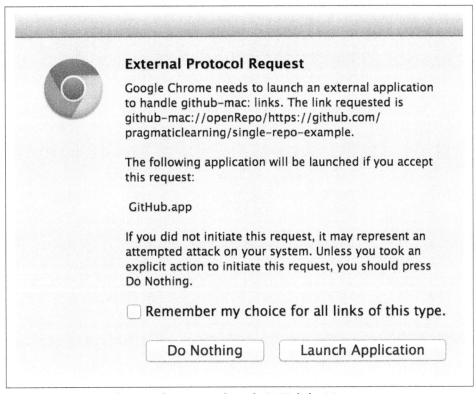

External Protocol Request

Google Chrome needs to launch an external application to handle github-mac: links. The link requested is github-mac://openRepo/https://github.com/pragmaticlearning/single-repo-example.

The following application will be launched if you accept this request:

GitHub.app

If you did not initiate this request, it may represent an attempted attack on your system. Unless you took an explicit action to initiate this request, you should press Do Nothing.

☐ Remember my choice for all links of this type.

Do Nothing   Launch Application

Figure 6-11. External protocol request to launch GitHub for Mac

You should allow the connection—in my case, I click the Launch Application button to launch GitHub for Mac and open a file explorer window, as shown in Figure 6-12.

Figure 6-12. Selecting a directory to clone a repo into

Select the directory you'd like to clone the repo into, click the Clone button, and Git-Hub for Mac will clone the repository for you. Once the repo has been successfully cloned, you should see a screen similar to Figure 6-13.

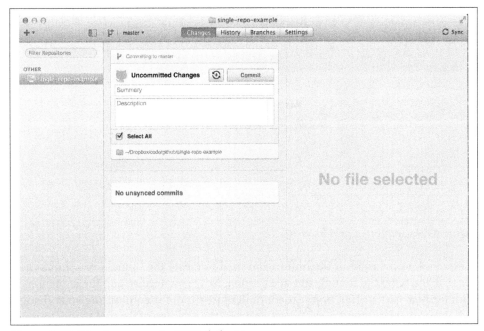

Figure 6-13. Viewing a repo in GitHub for Mac

At the top left is a + icon that you can use to create a new repository in a given directory or clone a repo from GitHub. Below that, the left panel shows a list of the repositories that you're working with locally, and it can be hidden by clicking the blue box
at the top of the page.

At the top of the screen, just to the right of the blue box is an icon that you can click
to create a new branch, and a drop-down list for selecting which branch you want to
be looking at and working on. Below that, when you select the default Changes tab,
you can see a text box where you would enter a commit message if you had changes
to commit.

Making a Commit Using GitHub for Mac

To make a new commit using GitHub for Mac, you probably want to start by creating
a new branch. In Figure 6-14 you can see that I'm creating a branch called "new_fea-
ture."

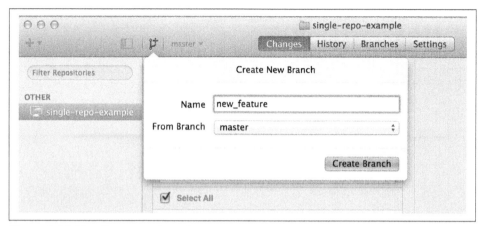

Figure 6-14. Creating a new branch

If you look to the right of the button you used to create the branch, you should now see that you're on the branch you just created. Now you need to add the content. Git-Hub for Mac isn't an IDE or a text editor. It's just a tool for committing your changes to Git, so you're going to need to use a text editor or some other tool to create a new file and put it in your project directory. I created a new file called *new_feature.html* and saved it in the project directory. Create a new file using a text editor, save it in the project folder, and then go back to GitHub for Mac. You should see your changes in a screen similar to Figure 6-15.

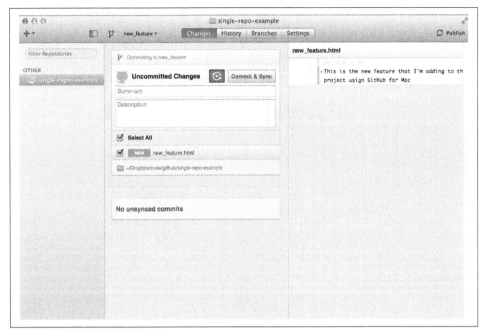

Figure 6-15. GitHub for Mac showing changes to be committed

Click in the Uncommitted Changes→Summary text box, enter a commit message, and then click the Commit & Sync button, and your changes will be saved to history and then pushed up to the remote repository.

If you do not have permission to push to the remote repository or if you are not signed into GitHub for Mac, you will see a screen similar to Figure 6-16.

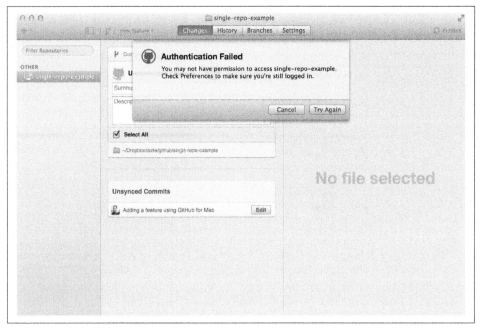

Figure 6-16. Authentication failed message

If that happens, check your credentials by opening the "Preferences - Accounts" window. Once you've successfully authenticated and confirmed that you are either an owner or collaborator for the project, you can click the green button to the right of the Commit button to sync your unsynchronized changes, uploading them to Git-Hub.

Viewing Changes in GitHub for Mac

There are three other tabs in the top bar of GitHub for Mac: History, Branches, and Settings. History shows you a list of commits on your current branch, as shown in Figure 6-17.

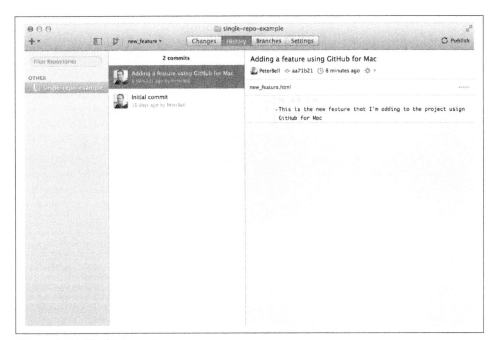

Figure 6-17. The history view

If you click the Branches tab, you'll see a screen similar to Figure 6-18.

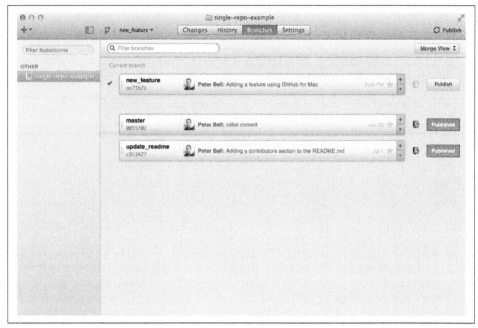

Figure 6-18. The branches view

This shows a list of all of the branches that you've created locally and all of the other branches that are on GitHub. Finally, if you click the Settings tab, you'll see a screen similar to Figure 6-19.

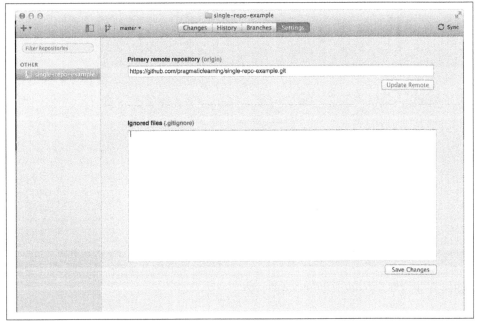

Figure 6-19. The settings view

In the Settings screen, you get the ability to configure two things. You could change the remote—something you're not likely to do very often. However, you can also tell Git to ignore certain files. Typically, you don't want to upload operating system files (like *.DS_Store* files from a Mac), IDE configurations, executable files, log files, or large binary files into a Git repository. If you put the names of any such files into "Ignored files," it'll add those to a *.gitignore* file that you can then commit and sync so nobody else on your project will accidentally commit those files either.

Hopefully, now you have enough information to be able to clone and commit to a repository locally should you need to do so using the GitHub for Mac application. Now we're going to look at the comparable application for Windows.

GitHub for Windows

To get a copy of GitHub for Windows, start by going to *https://windows.github.com/*. You should see a screen similar to Figure 6-20.

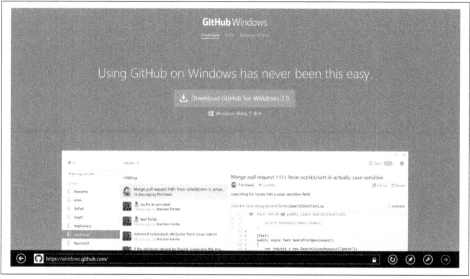

Figure 6-20. The GitHub Windows web page

Click the Download GitHub for Windows link and specify whether you want to Run, Save, or Cancel. You should click Run. You may see an application install security warning such as Figure 6-21. If so, just click the Install button, and the app will be downloaded and installed.

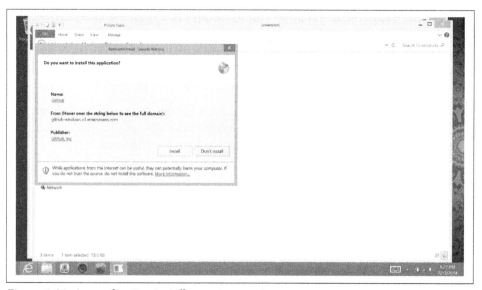

Figure 6-21. An application install security warning

Start up the GitHub for Windows app, and you should see a screen similar to Figure 6-22 welcoming you and asking you to sign in.

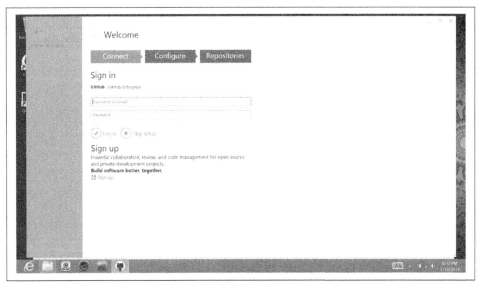

Figure 6-22. The setup wizard for GitHub for Windows

Enter your username or email and password for GitHub and click the "Log in" button. If you have enabled two-factor authentication to make your account more secure, you'll be asked to enter the code that was texted to your mobile phone, as shown in Figure 6-23.

Figure 6-23. Two-factor authentication

Once you've done this, you should see a screen asking you for some information to configure Git. In the first text box, you should enter the name you want to be known by, and in the second, enter the email address you'd like your commits to be associated with. Usually you'll enter your full name into the first box and the same email address you use for your GitHub account in the second one, as I've done in Figure 6-24.

Figure 6-24. Configuring your Git settings

Click the Continue button and you'll be taken to a screen that allows you to find local repositories. For now, just click the Skip button to go to the home screen in GitHub for Windows that looks like Figure 6-25.

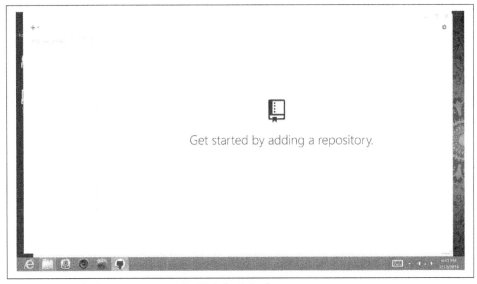

Figure 6-25. The home screen in GitHub for Windows

Once you've configured GitHub for Windows, don't worry if you get an email like the one shown in Figure 6-26 letting you know that "A new public key was added to your account." This is just GitHub letting you know that you've successfully connected Git-Hub for Windows to your GitHub account. It does that by adding a new public key that allows GitHub for Windows to connect to your GitHub account.

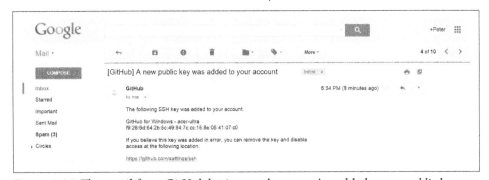

Figure 6-26. The email from GitHub letting you know you've added a new public key

Now that you've installed GitHub for Windows, go to a repository that you'd like to clone (download) and that you own or are a collaborator on. You can clone any pub-lic repo, but you won't be able to push your changes back up to GitHub unless you're either an owner or a collaborator. If you look at the bottom-right corner of the page, you should see the "Clone in Desktop" button, as shown at the bottom right of Figure 6-27.

Figure 6-27. A repo with the "Clone in Desktop" button

Click the "Clone in Desktop" button. The exact result when you click the button may depend on the browser and version that you're running. In Internet Explorer, I get the pop-up in Figure 6-28 asking whether I meant to switch apps. You should get something similar.

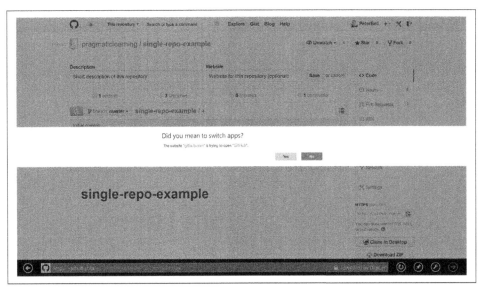

Figure 6-28. Confirming that you wanted to open GitHub

Click the Yes button to launch GitHub for Windows and open a file explorer window, as shown in Figure 6-29.

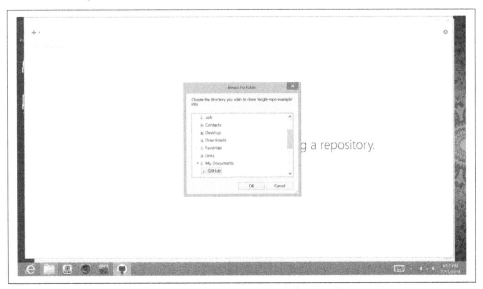

Figure 6-29. Saving your cloned repository in GitHub for Windows

Select the directory you'd like to clone the repo into, click the Clone button, and Git-Hub for Windows will clone the repository for you. Once the repo has been successfully cloned, you should see a screen similar to Figure 6-30.

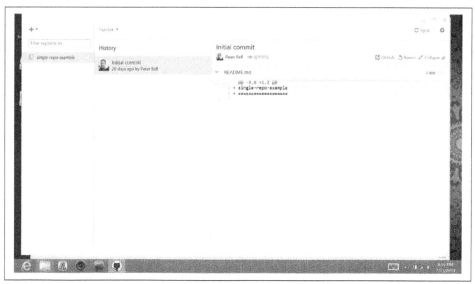

Figure 6-30. Viewing a repo in GitHub for Windows

At the top left is a + icon that you can use to create a new repository in a given directory or clone a repo from GitHub. Below that, the left panel shows a list of the repositories that you're working with locally.

At the top of the screen, just to the right of the blue box is a drop-down list that you
can click to select an existing branch or to create a new branch. Below that, you can
see a text box where you would enter a commit message if you had changes to commit.

Making a Commit Using GitHub for Windows

To make a new commit using GitHub for Windows, you probably want to start by
creating a new branch. In Figure 6-31, you can see I'm creating a branch called "win-
dows_feature."

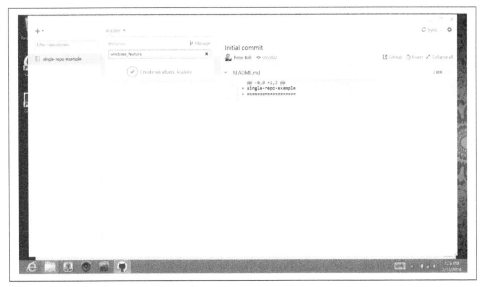

Figure 6-31. Creating a new branch

If you click the Create button below your new branch name, then look above where you created the branch, you should now see that you're on the branch you just created. Now you need to add the content. GitHub for Windows isn't an IDE or a text editor. It's just a tool for committing your changes to Git, so you're going to need to use a text editor or some other tool to create a new file and put it in your project directory. I created a new file called *windows_feature.html* and saved it in the project directory. Create a new file using a text editor, save it in the project folder, and then go back to GitHub for Windows. You should see a new "Uncommitted changes" message. Click it and you should see a screen similar to Figure 6-32.

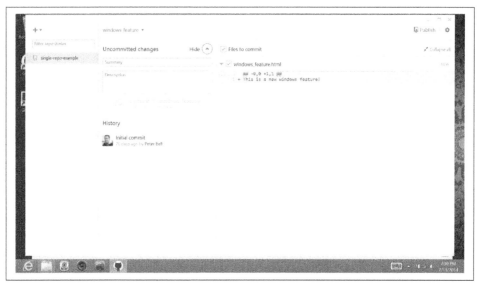

Figure 6-32. GitHub for Windows showing changes to be committed

Click in the Uncommitted Changes→Summary text box, enter a commit message, and then click the Commit & Sync button, and your changes will be saved to history. Then click the Publish button at the top right, and the changes will be uploaded to GitHub.

Configuring Command-Line Tools in GitHub for Windows

Sometimes it's useful to be able to use Git on the command line. If you want to be able to do that, the command-line tools are installed by default, but it's worth clicking the Settings icon at the top right of GitHub for Windows. A drop-down list will appear, as shown in Figure 6-33. Click the Options link.

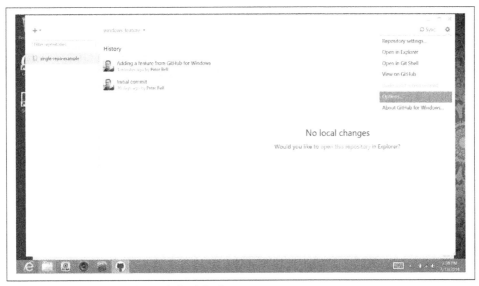

Figure 6-33. Settings in GitHub for Windows

When you click Options, you'll see a screen similar to Figure 6-34.

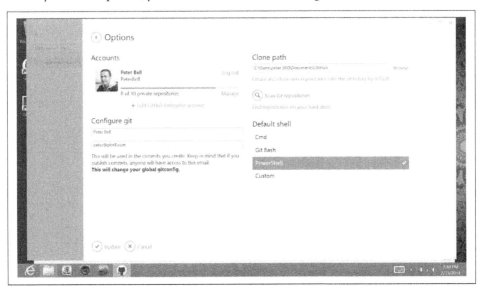

Figure 6-34. Options in GitHub for Windows

One change that's worth making is to change the default shell from PowerShell to Git bash. It means that when you launch Start→GitHub→GitHub Shell, it'll put you in a shell that will provide access to more applications that you might need such as vi (a text editor). Once you're done, click the Update button at the bottom left of the page to save your changes.

Hopefully, now you have enough information to be able to clone and commit to a repository locally should you need to do so using the GitHub for Windows application.

CHAPTER 7

Next Steps

We've covered a lot of ground in this book. We started by looking at how to view a project and then moved through the process of forking a project, making edits, and then collaborating on a single repository. We looked at how to create and configure a new repository and how to use the GitHub GUI clients to download and work on repositories locally.

For many people, this is all you'll need to know. The important next step is to practice until the skills become second nature and collaborating via GitHub becomes a natural way for you to work with teams of people on text-based files—whether source code or other projects.

There are some things that can only or best be done on the command line. For many people, you never need to make the jump to the command line, but if you're working on projects in Git all day, every day, it makes sense to learn how to use Git from the command line. Jon Loeliger and Matthew McCullough created a great book called *Version Control with Git* (O'Reilly), which would be a great next step if you wanted to learn more about using Git from the command line.

GitHub also provides a number of resources for learning more about both Git and GitHub. For more information, go to *https://training.github.com/*.

GitHub is going to become an increasingly important part of the workflow of many companies. This is a great time to get familiar with it. Best of luck with the journey!

Peter Bell
Brooklyn, NY
July, 2014

Index

About the Authors

Peter Bell is a contract member of the GitHub training team; the founder of Pragmatic Learning (*http://praglearn.com*)—an enterprise training company; the founder of the CTO Summit series and the Startup CTO School; a regular presenter at technical conferences; and an adjunct professor at the Columbia School of Business, where he teaches classes on digital literacy and Big Data. He teaches business people how to get software built successfully at Learn to Speak Geek! (*http://www.speakgeek.co*).

Brent Beer has used Git and GitHub for over five years through university classes, contributions to open source projects, and professionally as a web developer. He now enjoys his role teaching the world to use Git and GitHub to their full potential as a member of the GitHub training team.

Colophon

The animal on the cover of *Introducing GitHub* is a *Bare-tailed woolly opossum* (*Caluromys philander*), an arboreal species of marsupial also known as the white-eared opossum. This species is restricted to only moist forests, and can be found in Brazil, Bolivia, French Guiana, Guyana, Suriname, Trinidad and Tobago, and Venezuela. With its prehensile tail—which allows it to climb, balance, and grasp objects—the white-eared opossum is rarely, if ever, found on the ground and seldom found in the understory.

Ranging in weight from 140 to 390 grams, the female bare-tailed woolly opossum is typically smaller than males. It generally has soft and thick fur, which differs depending on the animal's habitat and location. It has a reddish-brown back with gray gradations along its flanks and a yellow-orange belly. It has a gray head with distinct dark-brown strips that run down the bridge of its muzzle and out from the dark-brown eye-rings to the nose. About a quarter of its tail has fur, the rest is furless and cream to dark gray or brown in color with brown or white spots.

The mating rituals of the bare-tailed woolly opossum is a bit of a mystery. Generally, individuals are solitary except when males court females. White-eared opossum have up to three litters per year, depending on resource availability. Females can have up to seven young at one time, averaging at around four young per litter in the wild; this, too, depends on resource availability. Bare-tailed woolly opossums have short gestation periods (24 days) and extended periods of parental care (up to 120 days of pouch time and 30–45 days in the mother's nest). Leaving the mother's nest is an important behavior, as demonstrated in captivity when young who have not been removed cannibalize their mother.

The bare-tailed woolly opossum is not listed as a species of concern, which is credited to its small size and adaptability to various types of neotropical forest. This could change as deforestation of neotropical regions continues.

Many of the animals on O'Reilly covers are endangered; all of them are important to the world. To learn more about how you can help, go to *animals.oreilly.com*.

The cover image is from *Meyers Kleines Lexicon*. The cover fonts are URW Typewriter and Guardian Sans. The text font is Adobe Minion Pro; the heading font is Adobe Myriad Condensed; and the code font is Dalton Maag's Ubuntu Mono.

Have it your way.

Lightning Source UK Ltd.
Milton Keynes UK
UKOW05f0620290416

273147UK00014B/103/P